FACES OF TRUTH

Stig Jørgensen

FACES OF TRUTH

AARHUS UNIVERSITY PRESS

Published with financial support from
The School of Law, University of Aarhus

AARHUS UNIVERSITY PRESS
Langelandsgade 177
8200 Aarhus N
Denmark
Fax 8942-5380

73 Lime Walk
Headington, Oxford OX3 7AD
Fax (01865) 75 00 79

Box 511
Oakville, Connecticut 06779
Fax (860) 945 9468

www.au.dk/unipress

ANSI/NISO
Z39.48-1992

PREFACE

I have developed a pluralistic theory of law in a number of previous works. Supporting the general relativity school of thought, this theory recognises that truth has many faces, and that particular truths are defined by the perspective or topic under debate. Thus I do not hold with any branch of relativity theory which implies that truth is irrelevant. On the contrary, it is my claim that we receive an answer to the questions we ask, but only if we use the relevant tools or methods.

Medieval science was teleological and scholastic, based as it was on the Aristotelian concept of matter which, in its turn, was based on the concept that all things have an ideal purpose or form which they strive to attain. Human nature was a combination of *zoon politikon* and reason, which implied both that man's ideal organisational structure was the Greek polis and that human reason was able to find the answer to all questions concerning reality and society. As it follows that truth is eternal, the task of science must be to undertake the interpretation of authoritative texts, resolving contradictions and filling in holes in the manner prescribed by the rhetoricians, thus creating a comprehensive system based on the fundamental rules for definitions, genus and species.

The Medieval study of law thus applied two methods of logic corresponding to its two manifestations, one scholastic, deriving from glossatorial Roman law based on *Corpus Juris* and one dialectic, deriving from canonical law based on canonical decrees. Later, the Sixteenth Century's Copernican revolution in the natural sciences gave rise to a mechanical cosmology based on causality which in turn was adopted by the philosophy of law, where it engendered a new school of natural law in tune with the new rationalism. David Hume's and Immanuel Kant's critiques of reason in the late 1700s led to the separation of

empirical and ethical knowledge and to an idealism which
stressed the dynamic element in ethics and law based on a historical approach to the use of sources and on a teleological legal
positivism.

While medieval science thus followed a mathematical-logical
approach, the Age of Enlightenment a mechanical-physical approach, and the Nineteenth Century a process-oriented approach
(e.g. the study of chemistry and electricity); the Twentieth Century saw the collapse of idealism caused by the emergence of
relativity theory around 1900. The reaction to this in ethics and
legal science thought took various manifestations. In France and
Germany various schools of phenomenology developed. In England the common sense approach gained strong support. In
Scandinavia and Central Europe, a number of 'realist' and
'logical' theories took shape, and pragmatism developed in
America.

On the one hand, these theories gave rise to an intuitionism,
which claimed that the human mind possessed a particular
objective faculty which made the acquisition of empirical and
ethical knowledge a simple process. On the other hand, logical
empiricists found the gap between empirical and ethical knowledge widening. Intuitionism made use of the same underlying
assumption as the idealism it had rejected, namely that there is
agreement between the empirical world and the mind, as either
the mind is projected on to the world (subjective idealism), or
the world, like the mind, is a logical construct (objective
idealism). Logical empiricism and related cognitive theories
claimed that scientific postulates can only be logically meaningful if they concern verifiable empirical phenomena.

If we assume that these assumptions are arbitrary and that
the external world, on the one hand, and cognitive processes
and language on the other, belong to distinct categories of logic,
we are facing a crucial epistemological problem which cannot be
resolved (as both Aristotle and Kant attempted) by merely
introducing the concept of *nous* (intuition) at the pre-scientific
level – the level where 'primary causes' or 'ideas' belong and
are processed into logical concepts for use in scientific analysis
and synthesis. It follows that unless we are prepared to accept

the idea that science is based on an unqualified intuition or is fundamentally arbitrary, we must make a new Copernican turnaround and leave behind 2000 years of fundamental rationalism, which saw our biological nature in the light of an *accessorium* to reason. We must take our point of departure in biology and start to consider our reason in the light of a tool on a par with our senses and other instrumental qualities, in other words as an element in the survival strategy of our genes.

Seen in this light, the recent instrumental language philosophy and teleological concept theory appear less strange. The hermeneutic approach becomes an indispensable instrument in both interpretation theory and the study of law, allowing us, as it does, to consider legal source materials in light of their purpose and the application of legal source materials as a pragmatic activity, culminating in the judicial decision and comprising a dialectic process between the interpretation and the qualification or labelling of reality through language with the general goal of establishing a 'desirable' decision. The fundamental values entering into this process are, on the one hand, the concern to safeguard the due process of law to which end predictability – and hence the systematic and logical application of the rule of law – is crucial, and on the other hand the concern to attain both this general goal and justice in any particular case. Plato and Aristotle drew attention to the fundamental problem arising from the application of a general rule to a specific event. It is necessary to harmonise general justice with the fundamental arbitrariness of the rule as applied to a particular situation, where the continuity of events is cut off by abstract and general rules. It is necessary, therefore, to harmonise strict justice (*isonomy*) with fair justice (*epeikeia, aequitas, equity, billighed*).

In the following chapters and in continuation of my book *On Justice and Law*, I present a more detailed account of anthropological epistemology and legal science, and draw out the consequences which such a pluralistic and fragmented view must have for the way in which we perceive the function of the law and issues surrounding the judicial decision.

CONTENTS

Preface   5

Contents   8

Modernism and Post-modernism   9

Language and Reality   14

Faces of Truth   24

Pluralism and Relationism   38

Pluralist and Relationist Legal Science   49

Tools and Methods in the Science of Law   55

Gadamer's Universal Hermeneutics   67

On Concepts in Law   76

The Theory of Dogmatics   88

Dogmatics and Empiricism   99

Contract and Delict   102

Proportionality   107

Law as a Standardising System   111

References   115

Index   118

MODERNISM AND POST-MODERNISM

'Post-modernism' is the name of a recent school of thought of some influence, particularly within the Arts. It is not entirely clear what the term stands for, as it presupposes the concept of 'modernism', a term with many meanings, but in the context of post-modernism, modernism is generally taken to mean faith in progress (the theory of evolution). Post-modernism is thus a 'critical' approach and is seen as a theory of interpretation. 'Deconstruction' is the tool used by post-modernist writers in the 'critical' interpretation of literature and art.

When this method is used to 'explain' a given interpretation, it will be unable to 'prove' anything, its only quality being that it *does not contradict* experience. Whether the theory is otherwise interesting depends, therefore, on the question of whether it is better able to explain the result than other metaphors and on whether it leads our thought astray in any other regard. For like other theories, models and analogies, metaphors are merely pictures which we use to slot experience into the structures of our conscious minds in order to make it 'understandable' (meaningful) to us.

In other words, 'post-modernism' and 'deconstructionism' are pragmatic concepts. Having no absolute validity, they are merely applicable or not applicable. If other more applicable models or theories are available, there is no particular reason to prefer post-modernism, if for no other reason than that it is an ambiguous and vague term and therefore apt to engender unfortunate associations. I shall mention the many earlier theories which aimed at finding 'the third way', the road between idealism and realism.

Like rationalism, idealism rests on the belief that human thought is the source of knowledge because, in the words of

Descartes, our ability to think makes knowledge certain, even if not true. A direct contrast to this conviction is Galileo's realism, which would have all things measurable, thus making knowledge true but not certain, because the laws of nature are incapable of proof, as Hume was later to say. Rationalist thinkers developed mathematics into an excellent tool for changing reality through technology, but could provide no certainty that all mathematical manifestations were applicable to reality. It follows that idealism's faith in progress was built on sand. Human thought is without limit, but it is not certain that our thoughts, the dream (the theory) can be realised.

Eighteenth Century rationalism was based on mechanical and physical causation in analogy with the new heliocentric Sixteenth Century cosmology, which also perceived social reality as a clockwork which was originally set and wound up by God and would continue to work for all eternity.

In contrast, the Nineteenth Century made use of the inherent process perspective derived from electricity and biology as the pattern for its theory of culture and historicism, including its theory of society and the law, which forms part of the theory of culture. The evolutionary perspective is transformed into an idealism which presupposes, like rationalism, that it is a simple process to transform the idea into reality and language into experience. The original 'subjective idealism' cancelled out the contradiction by postulating that our thoughts are projected on to the surrounding world, thus creating reality (Romanticism), while the later objective idealism presupposed that reason is real and that what is real is reasonable (Hegel).

The theory of the will (Schopenhauer and Nietzsche) had already rejected this model on the basis – to use Rudolf von Ihering's metaphor – that it is pointless to lecture a steam engine on motion, as an action without motive force is like an event with no cause. (Incidentally, the same fallacy recurs in modern language use, where it has become common to talk of the reason *behind* an event). Various attempts were made in the late Nineteenth Century to remove this idealistic assumption of identity between language and reality. The logical-positivist theory of the 20s-50s period was also based on this supposition, making verifiable statements the basic criterion in science, in contrast to 'metaphysics', thus presupposing identity between language utterance and the 'result of measuring', although these were necessarily members of distinct logical categories.

The theory of relativity from around 1900 made it clear that any knowledge arrived at depends on the measuring instruments. In other words, we only find answers to the questions we are able to ask by using the apparatus, and not all the answers at once. Holism is not a 'scientific' but an ontological concept. Spurred on by this, epistemology now sought analogous ways to create a new connection between language and reality.

French intuitionism (Bergson 1859-1941) presupposed a special mental apparatus in competition with the intellect, an apparatus which was instinctively able to rank the values in a given hierarchy such that it became possible to answer both theoretical and moral questions with certainty. Edmund Husserl (1964), the German heir to phenomenology, likewise presumes that it is possible to make an entirely spontaneous statement (*Wesenschau*) which breaks through all traditional ideas and hits upon and creates new knowledge through intuition. The same intuitionism underpins G.E. Moore's ethics (1903), which presupposes an objective system of ethics, while rejecting 'the naturalist fallacy', as does Axel Hägerström's similar 'realism' (1908).

In North America, John Dewey (1903) and William James (1907) had displaced the perspective from the present to the future in their Pragmatism, by making truth a function of the result of an action: if an action succeeds, it is right. The new British theory was, like its predecessor, tied to the concept of 'common sense' (Reid 1990), and the analytical Oxford version removed all boundaries and equated truth with 'common language use', thus turning ordinary language into a scientific yardstick (Hart 1961). The French 'existentialism' considers all choices to be 'true' if the person acting accepts 'responsibility' in full knowledge of the consequences of his choice, but it considers all laws and norms in the light of possible options and not as valid obligations.

What all these attempts to build a bridge between thought and reality have in common is the fact that they all refer to intuition in one form or another, and that they are otherwise sketches for or models of an answer which is tied to the ideology or mentality which formulated the theory. They also share a failure to provide an unambiguous 'explanation' of reality, the best that can be said in their favour being that none of them contradicts reality. To refer to 'intuition', 'ordinary language use', 'common sense', '*Wesenschau*', 'consequences' or 'choice' provides no better answer than the idealism which these theories want to leave behind. All they have achieved is merely to replace the evolutionary theory adopted by idealism with another 'launching pad' model.

A 'critical' or 'post-modern' theory thus departs from another political ideology than the liberal market economy, but without clearly indicating its political content. In contrast, a 'pluralistic', 'fragmented' or 'relational' epistemology expresses in an apolitical and non-metaphorical manner the fact, made necessary by relativity theory, that analytical and moral knowledge is culture-specific and intentional, presupposing as it does a model of knowledge (mentality, horizon) and an interest in knowledge.

This hermeneutic epistemology starts by postulating the absence of objective knowledge, but without making knowledge a subjective and private matter. This is in contrast to existentialism, which rejects the possibility of inter-subjective understanding along with the theories trying to objectify knowledge, such as Marxism and structuralism, the one operating with the concept of 'false consciousness' and the other with the concept of man's helpless dependence on a language which 'speaks' to him. Hermeneutics is an epistemology and language philosophy which openly recognises that knowledge is an interpretation of the empirical and social reality, and on this basis attempts to help us 'understand' knowledge, i.e. make it meaningful against a comprehensive systematic epistemological horizon.

We must realise, therefore, that our concepts are abstractions rooted in our interests and our strategy at the biological, genetic and social levels, such that our culturally created 'macro-society' counteracts our biologically designed 'micro-society'. Our intellect has been capable of creating a technological civilisation which is in opposition in many ways to the hunter/gatherer culture imprinted in our genes, and we must therefore allow our actions to be governed more by cool reason than by spontaneous feelings.

This comprehensive insight into the intentionality of language and the terms it uses to express the mix of our original 'natural' interests and acquired 'civilised' interests makes it clear that it is not enough for knowledge to be conservative in a *retrospective* sense: it must also be intentional in a *forward-looking* sense, and that in the final instance the face of knowledge depends on the model of society best able to realise the individual person's need for freedom and security. No epistemology or ethics can, however, be patented as the 'right' one, so it is important to avoid too many metaphorical terms, for they can lead our thoughts astray and beguile us into taking for granted the point we needed to prove. Models, analogies, metaphors and parables are methods of winning the recipient's understanding of new knowledge by using expressions with which the receiver is familiar, but with the attendant risk of misunderstandings arising.

When Christ was asked why he used parables when speaking to non-believers, he explained that while those already with faith knew the truth and could therefore understand his message directly, the use of parables – which referred to ordinary occurrences – enabled those without faith to gain a better understanding of his message.

LANGUAGE AND REALITY

1. Conceptions of language

The Book of Genesis tells us that Adam, *before* he had Eve to talk to, named (*dabar*) the animals and the birds. According to the Gospel of St. John: in the beginning was the Word (*logos*), then the Word was made flesh.

Here we have two completely different conceptions of the relationship between language and reality, a difference which can be traced back as far as we have evidence of man's awareness of this metaphysical question.

There is good reason to assume that the Genesis version is the older view, not only because the Old Testament was written 4-500 years before the Gospel according to St. John, but also because Genesis is in concord with the older Jewish mode of concrete thinking, whereas John's Gospel is a product of more recent abstract Greek thinking.

In his impressive 1976 work *The Origin of the Consciousness in the Breakdown of the Bicameral Mind*, Julian Jaynes analyses the corresponding development in Greek mentality as it is expressed *from* the naivety of the Iliad *to* Plato's idealism. According to Jaynes, two things about this old primitive thinking deserve particular note. Firstly it is the gods who act, not human beings, and secondly, feelings and actions are associated with concrete physical manifestations. Psyche is, for example, a breath, and temperaments are situated in certain glands and humours of the body such as blood, bile and phlegm. Primitive mentality is casuistic, collective and objective. Modern mentality with its generalising, individualistic and subjective qualities is created by the analytical and operational structure of the alphabet.

The conception of language as magic lies somewhere between these two extremes. The magic conception is concrete insofar as it perceives language to be a precise but purely mechanical code for bringing about a certain effect. Magic formulas are valid only if they are known and used quite accurately. We see this illustrated in the story of the sorcerer's apprentice, and reflected in modern day usage of terms such as 'Open Sesame' as a computer password. Greek sophism was the first philosophical school to distinguish between words and meaning, and this was the foundation of interpretation theory as it has remained until the present day: spirit and letter, will and declaration.

To the unreflecting mind – also of today – a thing and a name are inseparable. Speak of the Devil and he will appear. That is why in Danish we prefer to say 'speak of the sun'. Using deceptive words, we hope to deceive reality. The same belief underlies the commandment 'Thou shalt not take the name of the Lord thy God in vain', and the incentive to regard certain words as taboo, calling the wolf 'the grey one' and the bear 'the brown one'. The Pacific was so called in order to calm its wildness by means of a euphemism.

Magic and ritual words and procedures have played an important part in legal history. We know this from the development of Roman law, where *stipulatio* and *per aes et libram* changed from magic words into empty words, while *obligatio* changed from being a concrete tie between creditor and debtor with constraint on the person, to become the name of a legal institution, a fact to which the Swede Axel Hägerström paid very close attention. Similarly, the totem belief of North American Indians attributes to children the qualities of the totem animals after which they are named.

In one of his stories, the Danish writer Jørgen Nielsen tells of a boy who sees the world in a magic light, as all children do, and it makes him observe omens and perform ritual compulsive actions in order to bring about his wishes or prevent evil. The boy's mother suffers from a disease which, deep down, he knows is terminal, so he avoids mentioning the disease and tries to keep people around him from talking about illness and death. One day he is tired and inattentive, and he fails to escape before one of the neighbours expresses his sympathy for the mother.

Horror-stricken, he then realises that his mother's death is inevitable.

My colleague Kristian Ringgaard, Professor of Danish, told me an anecdote about a Frenchman who, pointing at the glass of water he was holding in his hand said, 'How very odd, the English call it 'water', the Germans 'Wasser', and it *is*, after all, only *de l'eau*!' Kristian Ringgaard also told me that his wife, who is Swedish, had taught their children to call him 'Papa' (the Swedish word for father), to the chagrin of his own mother, who believed that it was every man's right to be *called* 'Far' (the Danish word for father), since he didn't *become* a real father until he was called one in Danish!

2. Theories of language

In the Twentieth Century, we saw three major theories on the relationship between language and reality, none of which held out much promise of reality.

Structuralism, which dates back to the nineteen thirties and forties and was taken up again in France in the sixties, posits a degree of solidarity between expression and content, both of which are structured by means of abstract classifications and symbols. According to Structuralism, both expression and content are in principle arbitrary and decided by social convention, but once a word (e.g. 'water') has been thus chosen, it cannot readily be changed. Both expressions and content are abstractions, as the linguistic symbol does not combine a thing with a name, but a concept with an acoustic picture.

The second theory was put forward by the American chemical engineer Lee Whorf (1956). It was based on Whorf's study of Amerindian languages. These languages have none of the analytical character of European languages. They do not distinguish between subject and object or between the present, past and future tenses, which are expressed by means of intensity. According to Whorf, the very structure of language implies a metaphysics which forces upon the user of the language a certain perception of reality which is unconscious and inevitable.

Whorfianism flourished mainly in the forties and fifties. In

1957, the mathematician Noam Chomsky created a sensation with his theory of natural linguistic competence, implying a certain deep structure with a set of transformation rules (1957). These rules can be used to transform basic sentences into an arbitrary number of sentences in the surface structures of individual languages and, a level higher, into different language dialects. Language is a biological and genetically coded ability which must be developed like any other human ability and which develops gradually from the age of one. Miraculously, the final result of this development is a fairly correct use of language, even among children who have learned to speak from other children or from imperfect users of the language. Language development in children is thus more than a question of imitation, and Chomsky's theory has proved useful, especially in the field of genetic psychology, where Jean Piaget, for example, believed that children's linguistic ability can be shown to develop concurrently with their general psychological development from a concrete to an increasingly generalising conception of life and language (1936). Chomsky's theory does not, however, tell us much about the relationship between language and reality.

Modern anthropological psychology has gone still further. Drawing on findings in the fields of ethology and palaeontology, language development is explained as part of the tool and survival strategy of the human species. In this sense, the evolution of human intellect and language from a concrete and collective signalling system into a conceptual communication system must be seen as the development of a communication aid into a communication tool. Whether aid or tool, the idea of an 'I' and of 'time' is implied. Otherwise it would make no sense to retain a mere aid against the possibility of future need. Seen in this light, language is not an arbitrary formal sign system detached from reality, as the structuralists would have it, but part of the total conceptual apparatus developed by the human species as part of its survival strategy. The relationship of language to reality becomes instrumental, and the abstract words and concepts of language become teleological, serving as they do a human purpose.

3. Theories of knowledge

Aristotle's theory of knowledge was also teleological, assuming that man is a social animal (*zoon politikon*). Unlike other animals, however, man was imbued with reason, and this was his most important characteristic. According to Aristotle's metaphysics, every being will attempt to realise its nature, and this is the reason why human ethics must be judged in relation to an inherent purpose, which, on the other hand, is accessible to rational thought. Based on Aristotle's metaphysics, the theory of knowledge and moral philosophy remained teleological throughout the Middle Ages. This classical conceptual realism was, however, overthrown by Renaissance nominalism, which saw concepts as human tools which the individual may use as he chooses to change his physical world by means of technology and his social world by means of legislation.

The formation of this civilised mentality requires a distinction in the language structure between subject and object, an acting individual and a passive object. In fact, the history of writing emphasises the analytical alphabet as the system which best realises the analytical subject-object relationships of the Indo-European languages, in contrast to the weaker relationships and iconographic alphabets of the Asian-African synthetic languages. In a favourable geographic, social and economic climate, the combination of an analytical language and an analytical alphabet will, in fact, result in an individualistic perception of reality, technology and an instrumental ideology of law and legislation. The competition between king and church and the large and sparsely populated Western European area with its burgeoning urbanisation (civilisation) helped to create, as in classical Greece two thousand years earlier, the ideal conditions for an individualistic and democratic conception of reality and for the volitional contractual relationship between tender and consideration.

From the late Sixteenth Century, Galileo's and Descartes' theories of reality and knowledge were in competition. Galileo began with the outside world. Using refined measuring instruments, he wanted to make reality measurable, so a true but uncertain knowledge of the physical world could be established. Descartes, on the other hand, chose thought (*cogito ergo sum*) as his starting point in order to attain, if not true knowledge, at least certain knowledge about the physical world. Thus the foundation was laid for later centuries' distinction between realistic and idealistic theories of knowledge. From Descartes until the Eighteenth Century's natural law theory, rationalism assumed that it was possible to arrive at an objective knowledge of both the physical and the moral world by means of reason.

This belief in the possibility of objective knowledge was shattered towards the end of the Eighteenth Century by Hume's and Kant's critiques of reason. Hume pointed out firstly that it is individuals who think, not humanity; secondly, that it is our feelings and not our objective values which find expression in our moral and legal views; and thirdly, that causality is a product of the human consciousness, and not of the physical world. Kant's main contribution was to make knowledge part of the human mind from which we cannot distance ourselves. We have no bearings, however, unless we believe that the physical world is governed by the laws of causation (the realm of necessity) and that the inner moral world (the realm of freedom) is governed by our free will.

This dualism came to be reflected in Nineteenth Century epistemology, one characteristic feature of which was in fact the idea of some kind of concord between the physical world and thought. Subjective idealism assumed that thought constitutes reality, whereas objective idealism assumed that the physical world was arranged in a rational way (in terms of language), such that what is rational is real, and what is real is rational (Hegel). Around the turn of the Twentieth Century, however, this idealism gradually dissolved in attacks from several angles, with the general result that there is no correspondence between language and reality and hence no rational value system, only a hierarchy accessible through intuition.

In England, the old idealism was rejected by G.E. Moore, who based his theory of knowledge and ethics on an intuitive sense of truth and defended a kind of 'common sense' and ordinary language theory which had already been promoted by Thomas Reid one century earlier (1990). About the same time in Sweden, Axel Hägerström also rejected idealism, relying instead on a similar intuitive relationship between knowledge and the thing known – between language and reality. In Germany, Edmund Husserl developed a related so-called phenomenological epistemology and ethics in continuation of Henri Bergson's intuition theory, and in the United States, John Dewey and William James collaborated in developing a pragmatic theory of knowledge and moral philosophy, in which they used the realisation of a given purpose as the criterion of truth.

In the 1920s, logical positivism began its campaign against previous generations' idealist projection theory. Its purpose was to lay the foundation of certain scientific knowledge based on the assumption that our cognitive apparatus reflects the outside world, and that only that part of reality can become scientific knowledge which is verifiable through objective control and measuring instruments. It follows that ethics and natural law, along with religious phenomena, fell outside the province of science and must be grouped with feelings and beliefs under metaphysics. Hans Kelsen (1945) and Alf Ross (1953) were both legal positivists. They excluded justice as well as morality from jurisprudence; the law was nothing more than an element in the state apparatus and it was upheld only through its coercive measures. Ross went further than Kelsen, seeing law as a verifiable phenomenon and jurisprudence as statements of judges' ideology and behaviour, which in principle can be verified by reconstructing judicial decisions and their grounds.

The weakness of logical positivism as a theory of science is its confused attitude to the relationship between language and reality, assuming as it does the existence of an objective language. *Hermeneutic* theory denies the existence of an objective language or an objective description. Following Martin Heidegger's phenomenology (1927) and Ludwig Wittgenstein's later philosophy (1953), it sees language and its concepts as teleological, i.e. formed in accordance with human purposes and values. The Hermeneutic theory reminds us that the same phenomenon can be labelled in different ways (e.g. 'terrorist' or 'patriot'), depending on the attitude of the language user to the phenomenon.

The hermeneutic circle represents an insight into a fundamental obstacle to knowledge: One cannot *understand* a part of a whole without knowing this whole, and one cannot understand a whole, or its object, without knowing its elements. The Lilliputs were unable to make a record of Gulliver's belongings as they did not know firearms and smoking. The essence of knowledge, in fact, lies not in describing but understanding the physical world. The physical world should not be – and cannot be – described; it should be labelled according to an existing value system which can be more or less universal and more or less explicit. A 'description' is thus determined by its context and the 'forum' which it addresses.

In his 1953 thesis *Om oplevelse af andres adfærd* (On the Perception of Other People's Behaviour) the Danish psychologist Franz From demonstrated that a person's behaviour can be described only in intentional terms, because the representation of behaviour, or movements, in a physical system of co-ordinates would be both complicated and uninformative, just as from a distance it may be difficult to tell whether a person is threatening with a pistol or just smoking a pipe.

A hermeneutic theory of knowledge need not be relativistic, as how phenomena are labelled is not unimportant. It would be more appropriately labelled relationistic or pluralistic. This means that a description or evaluation must be made in relation to some particular value system and not by arbitrarily drawing on different systems, and indeed 'Relationism' is another name for the Hermeneutic school of thought.

4. Judicial decisions

It is clear that the theories of knowledge and language outlined above must affect our understanding of the problems of jurisprudence and judicial decision-making. If we cannot *describe* reality, the main problem involved in the application of the law cannot be the interpretation of a given legal material in relation to some legal facts but, on the contrary, to frame or label the given facts in relation to the legal material which *may* be applied, and then to decide whether it *should* be applied. If the facts have been labelled using the language of the rule of law, it is quite a simple matter to draw the logical conclusion from the major premise of the rule and the framed minor premise. In the world of reality, however, the outcome of this process is not a logical *conclusion*, but a psychological *decision*.

In the progress of every law case, several psychological decisions will be made in order to perform the required language qualification or labelling of facts such as evidence and assessment of evidence, and the legal qualification or framing of these established facts in terms of the relevant law rules. To this should be added an assessment of the intentions which are the primary content of any rule of action, and of the consequences normally attendant upon the various possible interpretations. In other words, the judicial decision is the result of a dialectic of teleological and pragmatic 'interpretations'.

5. Conclusion

The purpose of this long explanation of underlying issues in the application of law is to demonstrate that from time immemorial, people have been aware of the fact that the relationship between language and reality is more problematic than we often tend to think. Aristotle was well aware of the difference between *analytika priori* and *analytika posteriori*: between the certainty with which conclusions may be drawn within a given language system and the difficulties involved in inserting reality and values into a language system capable of producing certain conclusions only in the form of apodictic and dialectic syllogisms. As far as social phenomena are concerned, 'Topics' is the place to find arguments for rational decisions (conviction), whereas 'Rhetoric' is the arsenal for irrational decisions (persuasion).

The present cross-disciplinary approach to epistemology and linguistics, on the one hand, and anthropology and psychology on the other, has taught us that language is not only an integral part of the human cognitive apparatus, but also a part of the tool system which the human genes have evolved as part of their survival strategy. It follows that we cannot possibly understand the function of language without knowing its purpose. Both idealism and realism contain part of the truth, but not the whole truth. True, our knowledge is determined by the possibilities and limitations of our cognitive apparatus, and our understanding of reality is subject to these reservations. Nevertheless, reality exists and must be named, and we do so according to our interests and intentions. These interests, however, are neither subjective nor objective, but more or less intersubjective, ranging from almost entirely objective (universal) to almost entirely subjective (personal likes and dislikes). This insight renders the judicial decision problematic, since it relegates the interpretation of the legal materials in terms of general rules of interpretation, of language and of law to a position of much less importance. The principal purpose becomes instead *to describe the present facts* in such a manner that they correspond to the result of the interpretation, naturally adopting a process involving a dialectic interplay between interpretation and description. It is not possible to subject the framing of law to the same controls as those available in the interpretation of law, the process of which has been refined over thousands of years in the interest of law and order.

The object of these desultory remarks is mainly to sound the alarm against the arbitrary nature with which facts are formally described, often without this being noticed by either experts or involved parties, facts which cannot be described but only labelled or framed because language and reality are distinct logical categories. The task of the judge may be compared to that of a magician or manipulator: he performs his tricks with reality while distracting the attention of the audience by making them focus on something else. There is little point in installing an ingenious technical system in front of your property in order to protect it as long as you leave a barn door open at the back.

FACES OF TRUTH

1. Faces of truth

Accepting the consequences of the collapse of positivism and the relativity of knowledge, post-modernism – so-called – has taken steps to revive a pluralistic and relational approach to the external world. The main task is no longer to describe the world, but rather to interpret events and actions taking place in the world.

As early as the fifties, André Gide's *School for Wives* and Lawrence Durell's *Alexandria Quartet* anticipated this insight into the 'intentionality' of knowledge, i.e. its cultural determinism and perception of the recipient's expectations and mental universe. In the half century since, this insight has become far more radical, forcing us to abandon the classical supposition that knowledge is rational. The insight which palaeontological findings have given us into our close genetic relationship with chimpanzees has forced us to perform a Copernican revolution in our understanding of the connection between mind and knowledge. The human mind is not, as we believed, the primary force in relation to knowledge; rather, the human mind is a tool employed by the genes in their strategy to secure the survival of the species and hence of the individual.

The consequence of this is that we must relinquish our belief in a 'rational' explanation of individual human lives, and likewise our belief that we can explain and understand a person's actions with reference to his own ideas and motives. What Freud called the 'subconscious' and Jung the 'collective subconscious' are poetic terms for the fact that most of our values and behavioural patterns are tied to the reflex system of our genes, which controls most of our actions by circumventing our conscious minds. In 1968, Anthony Storr claimed in *Human Aggression* that human reason accounts for no more than a couple of percentages of the whole being, a proportion corresponding precisely to the difference between human genes and the genes of chimpanzees.

Following a historical philosophical outline, I shall illustrate this theoretical insight by an analysis of two literary works of current interest, Allan Massie's *Shadows of Empire* (1997) and John Banville's *The Untouchable* (1997).

2. The eyes that see

Although the debate on whether man is spirit or matter has raged throughout human history, there has always been tacit agreement that each of us has an inherent purpose. Since classical Antiquity, human reason has always been considered the hallmark of human nature, irrespective of whether divine or human reason was placed in the centre.

Plato began with the idea, which was then projected on to the external world, while Aristotle saw people as social and rational beings. Although Aristotle thus stressed human zoology as important for understanding, it was nevertheless reason, comprising thought and language, which was the decisive element. Like Plato and the pre-Socratic philosophers, he saw all values, truth, beauty and goodness as governed by the same measure. Socrates expressed the Greek ethics in the following piece of advice: 'If you look deep into yourself, you will find the truth about the good'. 'Know thyself' was the motto above the door to the oracle of Delphi.

This kind of rationalism, which sees the good as a matter of reason, came to dominate medieval theology and ethics, not least after Thomas Aquinas had elevated Aristotle to the position of leading philosopher in the late 1200s. As the Enlightenment's natural law theory continued to build on the same view, it is understandable that our moral and political thinking takes its theoretical starting point in the concept of democracy, defined as a reasonable debate among enlightened persons, although it was evident as early as the late Nineteenth Century that in reality it was little more than a power struggle among interests.

True, the rationalism of the Age of Enlightenment had been replaced by the Nineteenth Century's idealism, but the result was still the same. Reason governs our knowledge of the external world. The Romantics had seen nature as a reflection of human thought, while the later Hegelianism assumed the existence of an intrinsic logic in nature, which makes it a simple matter to understand how we come into contact with the external world, it being on the same wavelength as the human mind.

Nevertheless, the opposite thought was also alive, as we see from the well-known Latin maxim *Navigare necesse est; vivere non est necesse*. According to legend, this sentence was Pompeius's answer to the Roman captains who were unwilling to risk their lives in the Mediterranean storms in the winter season, despite the necessity of supplying grain from North Africa to feed the population of Rome.

But it was not until the turn of the Twentieth Century, when the dominant idealism collapsed in the face of new insights into the relativity of knowledge, that ethics gave up the attempt to find rational reasons for the 'sovereign expressions of life'. It was clear by then that both theoretical and practical (moral) knowledge were dependent on teleological (i.e. purposeful) interests, and that these must be found through intuition. Reason dictates that you must sail if you have decided to live.

Although it has been known since the 1600s that it is the earth that is revolving around the sun, we continue to speak in both poetic and practical terms of sunrises and sunsets, and although we know very well that the clouds and the wind are both effects of low pressure systems, it makes 'sense' to speak of the wind sweeping the sky clear of clouds. In our daily language we can also continue in the same manner to speak of actions as good or evil, although we know that it is not necessary to live.

We speak spontaneously of warm, soft and round curves in contrast to cold, hard and sharp edges, and in so doing we transfer our feelings as living beings to aesthetic and moral statements. When we also speak warmly of our social attitudes to family and friends and transfer them to society as a whole, we are similarly displaying our social animal quality (*zoon politikon*), the very essence of human nature as Aristotle, Medieval ethics and the Enlightenment's natural law philosophers saw it.

This perception of the relationship between nature and morals is now gaining support from philosophy in general, which sees our decisions and actions as part of our total biology. We must see language as an extension of the conceptual apparatus by which we find our bearings, and in conformity with which we act 'rationally' in the sense that it improves the chance of survival for ourselves and our species, i.e., our genes. It follows that our actions are not a tool for our reason, our thought and the language in which we describe and communicate with the external world; rather, our reason is part of the strategy which our genes have 'chosen' for their own survival.

Compared with other animals, this is, on the other hand, a dramatic difference, as other animals have not developed the ability to develop and transform abstract notions, or to communicate information about the external world in a language which is more than a system of signals. The development of this human consciousness about itself and the external world has been so extensive that it has come to dominate human consciousness, so that we have put the cart before the horse. Our biology is not a tool to be used by the mind (the ideal, the soul, the reason); quite the contrary, it is a highly refined means by which the human species has become ruler of the earth.

The result of this insight is not that ethics can be explained by reference to our desires, as earlier 'naturalists' held. Their view is as fallacious as the view that ethics can be explained by reference to our reason. Morality does not derive from, and cannot be derived from, custom or natural law, as knowledge and morality belong to distinct categories of logic. Scientific knowledge is based on the laws of nature, while morality is inferred from the freedom of the will. It was Immanuel Kant who introduced this logical distinction between the realm of

necessity and the realm of freedom two hundred years ago, and
nobody has yet been able to remove it.

The obverse side of this insight is that we cannot uphold a
naive realism or positivism which claims that the moon has the
colour which moons should have, and that it is both possible
and simple to give an objective description of the world, and
thus to prove how it is constituted. If language is part of our
survival and perception apparatuses, it is only able to 'express'
what is already present in our genes, and it will therefore be
coloured by our natural and cultural preferences and decisions.
If language is a tool, it means that we use it not only to
'describe' things, but also to 'do something' to things with.

A classical example of this pluralist language theory is the
labelling of the people of the underground movement during
the German occupation of Denmark during the Second World
War. They were simultaneously called 'freedom fighters' and
'terrorists', a situation which recurred in Kosovo. Similarly,
when I look out of my window, I am unable to determine
immediately whether I see a forest or a park. There are trees in
both, but how many, and how densely should they stand?

It may be that many Danish people – and perhaps most –
will shrug their shoulders at this kind of 'philosophy', which
merely serves to confirm the popular belief in the Danish
humourist Storm Petersen's definition of science: 'A difficult
way of saying what everybody already knows'. There is much
truth in this bit of irony, but also a danger, one which Ludvig
Holberg warned against in his *Erasmus Montanus*. For if we look
closely, the tragedy of the story was that while Rasmus was
right in his construction of world order, and the parish clerk, the
peasants and all the people were wrong, Rasmus lost the
argument because he was a petty-minded pedant trying to
elevate himself above the common people instead of raising
them to a higher level of insight.

Although we can see with our own eyes that the horse is
pulling the cart and that the man is pulling a gun out of his
pocket, we don't *know* whether the cart may be pushing the
horse, or whether it may be a pipe the man has in his pocket.
We make assumptions when trying to *interpret* a series of

events, and among these are necessarily a number of probability calculations based on experience and insight into regular occurrences.

'I'he latter example, which is borrowed from Professor Franz From (1953), shows with all clarity how cautiously one must treat the explanations given by the parties to, and witnesses, in a court case. Individual explanations will be coloured not merely by the person's interest in winning or losing the case, but first and foremost by the person's experiences and perceptual universe.

We often see what we expect to see, and we have always known that what is seen depends on who saw it.

3. Shadows of Empire

Present day intellectuals call it deconstruction when the rest of us prick the balloons or puncture the myths. The British writer Allan Massie has written several historical novels, including one on Augustus, *The Memoirs of the Emperor* (1986). The topics of these books cover the transition of Rome from the city state's republican innocence to the impenetrable power relationships of a world power. The book in which Augustus is the main character, illustrates that – like a modern-day Richard Nixon – he did what was necessary, but was cunning enough to veil his despotic powers under the mask of the old republican virtues.

In his most recent book, *Shadows of Empire* (1997), Massie deals with the British myth of empire, which finally dies long after the empire itself had perished during and after the Great War. It is Massie's point that the interwar period was like a middle age, an interim period or pupal stage in which England or Great Britain underwent the metamorphosis from empire to island state offstage, dominated in part by the aristocracy's sense of *noblesse oblige* and a social democratic welfare model.

The narrator, an independent journalist with roots in the fringes of the old aristocracy, writes a kind of family saga. He is, despite his book, a kind of voyeur, or like Robert Musil a man with no qualities, an observer who is never fully engaged in life or politics, in contrast to his ancestors who were active in business and culture, and his siblings who each make their own choice with catastrophic consequences for themselves and their surroundings. The story is mainly set in Berlin and Paris in the years 1931-48, and the author or narrator – the two merge imperceptibly at times – rounds off the family and national history in Glasgow in 1984, while the family scenes play mainly at Blanket, the parental mansion near London.

It is no accident that the father, who inherited a fortune from his Scottish shipbuilding family and whose royalties continue to maintain his family in its upper-class life styles long after his death, appears as the author of conventional dramas and crime novels, or that he stubbornly continues to uphold the British imperial aristocratic and rationalist myth with just that touch of nostalgia and self-pity which, the narrator believes, is a condition of public success, or that he has had considerable box-office success. From his Scottish puritan ancestors the father also inherited the Protestant work ethic 'make something', built into the Nineteenth Century's Victorian idealism. It was this that created the empire builders, the officers, engineers and administrators who made the global network hang together, backed by a navy which 'ruled the waves' and a commercial fleet which secured the financial exchanges of raw materials from the Dominions with finished goods from England and contributed to the development of technical infrastructures in the colonies.

While the older generations' achievements had been in the real world, the father's achievement was restricted to the world of fiction and consisted in the reproduction of the aristocratic myth, with an awareness, however, that the young generation who marched to the war in 1914 had held different convictions from those of the present generation. While the young men of 1914-18 had fought for an idea, the youth of 1939-45 were representatives of the democratic egoism and morality, an analysis which leads two of his sons to the decision to betray their 'country', one becoming a communist and diplomat and the other a Nazi sympathiser in continental Europe, where he makes a film during the German occupation of France. Both make their choice based on a rejection of the American materialism without nurturing any warm feelings, one for the working classes and the other for the vulgarity of Nazism.

A third brother builds a career for himself in Asia, interrupted by a traumatic interlude as a Japanese prisoner of war, but disintegrates eventually in corruption and alcohol, while a sister who is the only person with any vitality among them, for rational reasons and to save the family mansion marries a rich admirer after the death of her handsome and naive husband early in the war. The narrator himself lives his vague and lifeless existence as an observer and analyst without ever taking a personal stand on any of the political and personal events happening around him, and he finishes his narrative as a creaky old bachelor momentarily enlivened by the presence of a young girl and her interview.

Through the narrator's account and his reflections on the family fortune, we piece together an analysis of the recent history of England and Europe. We are forced to see parallels between Neville Chamberlain's appeasement policy in 1938, Pétain's Vichy and Danish prime minister Scavenius's collaboration politics. Neither England, France nor Denmark had the courage to respond adequately to Hitler's provocation, partly because – whether wilfully or by negligence – everybody underestimated Hitler and his intentions, and in part because the slaughters of the Great War were still painfully vivid in the memories of the thirties. Hitler could, perhaps, have been stopped by Hindenburg, possibly at the time of the occupation of the Rhineland, but not in 1938 or 1939 ('... all the same, to go to war in order to compel the Sudetenland Germans to remain part of a Republic which they didn't wish to belong to – that made no sense?' (p. 185). 'We went to war to defend Poland. And now Poland's occupied. So what are we fighting for? Can anyone answer me that?' (p. 204).

Neither is the reader shown Winston Churchill as anything other than a 'warmongering' overgrown baby, who worked zealously to dismantle the empire, despite all his rhetoric and fuss (Gallipoli, Churchill's catastrophic venture in the Great War, had not been forgotten). Like the Danish resistance movement, de Gaulle is seen not as a force which inflicted any note-worthy losses on the powers of occupation, but as the symbol which ensured the French people forgiveness and a seat at the table among the superpowers in the political and legal settling of scores after the war.

In the eyes of the narrator, this is why the legal aftermath of the war was so particularly violent and ruthless against small and great collaborators in France, for behind the narrator's expressionless face and inner vacuum hides miraculously a moral sense which makes him pity the puny, ordinary grey men in Nuremberg and sicken at the thought of their execution in the autumn of 1946. This is why he has more than a little respect for Goering, because he was the only one to show some personal calibre and a clear recognition of the situation, but especially because he cheated the hangman. 'Do you identify with the dock or the bench? For me, the dock, every time', he states rhetorically.

The narrator subsequently finds this 'moral sense' during a recreational visit to a school friend and friend of his youth, who is a medical practitioner in Scotland and is keenly engaged in the great health reform which Attlee's social democratic govern-ment is in the process of introducing. For social democracy is not an ideology as the old imperial myth or the new com-munism was, it is merely a new morality, as the friend explains in one of their late night discussions.

If there is any moral to be drawn from this dialectic novel at all, it must be the dislike of any ideology, including the Ameri-can species of market-oriented capitalism. In the eyes of the narrator, Margaret Thatcher is no modern hero.

What is left? One may well ask, after the gradual reduction of England from imperial centre to a second-rate island state which has difficulty finding its place in the new Europe (and not 'Neuropa', as the lost brother had believed, and to which he had tried to adapt). Perhaps England was reduced to its natural size, as was said of France after the death of de Gaulle, and returned to its identity before imperialism, when reason was not the only voice heard. Certainly towards the end of the book, the Romantic irrational element raises its voice, as the narrator is reminded of the Romantic philosopher and poet Ludwig Tieck who let the prince in one of his dramas order that the piece be played backwards when he found himself unable to complete his adventurous journey. One senses that the factual and practical female realism is the future truth, as the narrator tells the young female interviewer that she should rather, perhaps, have spoken to his practical sister, whom she would have appreciated.

In an ironic postscript we hear of a young author who is planning to write a drama on Alistair, the least responsible of all the family members, who failed either because he was his father's favourite or because everything came easily to him, thanks to his superficial charm, or because he was genetically predestined to become a loser, as he was a man without qualities, even more so than the narrator. Thus several of the book's characters begin to doubt at some stage whether he really exists when he is not in company with somebody else.

The comedy can begin anew, because it is always the lost sons who inherit the kingdom and who become the main characters in the human species' mythological dramas. It turns out that this anti-hero died as an emigrant in Argentina, not heroically or justly, but as the victim of a banal jealousy drama. 'I suppose I can give my manuscript to the boy and send him away. Tell him to make what things he will of it', the narrator muses, ending his story and the book with the rhetorical question: 'Or shall I take him up the valley to the ruined keep and show him desolation?'

4. The Untouchable

Nothing is as it seems!

This insight into the relativity of understanding is part of traditional common knowledge, but it only became part of epistemological theory in the Twentieth Century. It is the same old story. We only become 'conscious' of something long after we have reacted to it.

Our automatic reflexes provide an elementary illustration of the bipartite nature of knowledge by which the purely vitalistic reaction to an event in the medulla oblongata (hypothalamus) is separated from the conscious registration and processing (hippocampus) of it. 'Once bitten, twice shy', but even before the pain registers consciously, we have withdrawn our hand, and our eyelids close even before a foreign body touches the eyeball.

This bipartite nature of our cognitive apparatus reflects our evolutionary history and reveals the line of causality between sensory apparatus and conscious mind. It cannot possibly be the case that our sensory apparatus has developed to serve our conscious mind. Rather, our conscious mind must be a later development in response to our genes' collective strategy.

Since classical antiquity, the study of ethics has been based on the assumption that reason (our conscious mind) is the form and nature of humankind, and that by using our reason we can gain knowledge not only of the external world but also of what is morally right. Increasing insight into human nature, with its twin elements of biology and reason, made the matter more complex, and towards the end of the Eighteenth Century, Immanuel Kant already proved that theoretical knowledge is impossible without the existence of causality, and practical or moral knowledge is impossible without the existence of free will.

It was not until the early Twentieth Century, however, that the consequences of this insight began to penetrate into epistemology and ethics, when – after the collapse of idealism around the turn of the century – the relativity theory and pluralist epistemology turned the relationship between the individual and knowledge upside down. The hermeneutic teleological epistemology and language philosophy has managed at one stroke to stress the species-specific element in both cognition and language, while the instrumental element in human language concepts provides clear proof of the subjective and inter-subjective element in cognition.

This element of instability in our recognition of truth and morality may be recognised in several 'post-modern' writers, of whom the Irishman John Banville is arguably the most consistent. In *The Newton Letter* (1982) we are already made to see the fragile nature of knowledge and memory in the account of a writer who, while at work on a book on Isaac Newton and while puzzling on Newton's strange silence which lasted 34 years from the publication of his work on mathematical-physical causation and until his death, becomes increasingly distracted by the complex ties among the family members of his temporary landlord.

In his later novel *The Book of Evidence* (1990), a tour de force account of an accidental murder and the evidence of it prove to be vague and contradictory because of the murderer's/author's unstable mind and his desire to confess in order to be punished as a moral person. How can you be guilty if knowledge is subjective and susceptible of several interpretations? How can you be responsible if you are not master of your own actions? The problem thus shifts from a legal universe to a religious one.

On the one hand, it is the 'universality' of language and knowledge which paralyses the characters, bound as they are by the laws of nature, and on the other hand, the incapacity of science to answer the question of what essential moral insight is, an insight which can only be grasped in intercourse with so-called common people who 'know' what is right without being able to explain themselves, or who provide reasons which are often wrong or irrelevant.

John Banville has recently published a new novel portraying the same doubts concerning our human capacity for gaining rational insight into 'facts' with our attendant uncertainty in the making of moral 'choices'. The name of the book is *The Untouchable* (1997) and the ostensible topic is the life of the fourth of Britain's gang of four spies, Burgess, Maclean, Philby and, finally, Blunt, who was not disclosed until he had achieved and held a high academic and social position for many years as the curator of the Queen's paintings.

This is not a biography or documentary account in any traditional sense, but a fiction, as indicated by the fictive names and the subjective form in which narrator and author melt into one in an autobiography, which the reader is left to believe will be posthumous as the narrator presumably commits suicide when he realises that he, who thought he had betrayed his country, his wife and his friends, has in fact been exploited and betrayed by his surroundings.

Not only does his life end in public disgrace with the withdrawal of all privileges and comforts, but his entire self-perception and self-respect vanish when he finally realises that it was his closest friends who deceived him and informed on him. One or two of them may in fact be the father of his children, while the other – his hero and later brother-in-law – is the person who used him, firstly by indirectly recruiting him to spy for the Soviet Union in Cambridge in the thirties, later by pretending not to be involved, and finally by informing on him to the authorities.

During all these years he has lived in an illusion of having been in control of his life, well capable, thanks to his emotional stoicism, of managing in life despite its risks, not only from his spying activities but also as a homosexual. In reality, however, he has been nothing but a naive and useless puppet in other people's bigger games, not only unimportant to the 'enemy' who had other and bigger fish to fry, but also to the authorities, who had always known all his 'secrets'. The worst blow, and the one which makes him consider suicide, is, however, the revelation of his friend's double game, and the fact that the reason for this was the friend's lack of faith in his strength, and not least the knowledge that this friend and hero is the person who sold him to the authorities because they want something in return for continuing to cover up the main case in the interest of both parties.

How much 'truth' there is in the story (apart from the external framework) I cannot say, but the *zeitgeist* and its expressions in political and ideological polarisations are caught as precisely as in Allan Massie's *Shadows of Empire*, which also portrays the paralysis which seized the English upper classes when the post-World War I era dawned on Britain with an atmosphere of collapse and an unattractive choice between the vital and vulgar American democracy and the just as vulgar Soviet Communism, with fascism cast in the role of common enemy, so to speak.

Just as Massie's main character is a kind of voyeur, so Banville's is pre-eminently an aesthete who believes he is a man of action, and just as Massie's, he plays with life, and is allowed to play with life. Like Massie, Banville uses a biography or a hypothetical biography as his framework. Attempting in vain to catch the 'subjective' life, he is constantly overtaken by the objective life, the history written by our genes for the survival of the species.

As in Banville's earlier books there is a religious dimension in the description of depravity in the academic elite's empty and hedonistic lives, in which a latent need to be punished for the betrayal becomes the motivating force behind the betrayal. The atheist is the most religious of all. The pathos and childishness of this is shown in the narrator's manic fixation on a painting, the *Death of Seneca* by Poussin, showing an idealised tableau of Seneca's death, after his former student, the emperor Nero, had ordered his suicide. This 'meek' acceptance of the conditions of life is the narrator's formal ideal and maxim, although we repeatedly witness a simply childish emotional rage in him, at one and the same time the adrenaline is high which is the reward for his double life in a double sense – as spy and gay – and his snivelling collapse in front of the wife whom he has left and who must console him by telling him the truth of his self-delusion.

The title of the book contains another double irony: the main character's stoicism is a front and his untouchability arises from the fact, unknown to himself, that nothing is the way he thinks it is.

In Danish literature, the novels by Svend Åge Madsen, *Sæt verden er til* and *Se dagens lys*, not to mention his very first work *Otte gange orphan* have pre-empted this uncertain and fragmented consciousness with traces of compulsive behaviour caused by our species-specific cognitive and reflexive background which, in the words of John Banville, causes our attempts at catching the subjective 'story' to be constantly overtaken by the objective 'history' which is written by our genes.

PLURALISM AND RELATIONISM

1. Prognosis

Law can be approached from different angles and thus from the points of view of different parties' interests. O.W. Holmes (1981) drew attention to the fact that in considering the law to be a set of prophesies of future concrete judicial decisions, American realism was 'the bad man's law'. It is only those who are interested in finding out how far they can go who are interested in knowing the probability of the public power apparatus being turned against them. American realism, however, also reflects the fact that the judge is a dignitary in the Anglo-American legal tradition, so that it is natural to seek the criterion for the law's existence in the actions of the judge.

2. Command – rule

H. Hart's theory of law (1961) differs on this point from the Anglo-American tradition while also removing itself from Kelsen's continental theory of power (1945). The command theory of absolutism thought out by Thomas Hobbes (1974) was taken over by the theory of volition in the Nineteenth Century, which was then taken over by John Austin (1832), whose theory was rejected by Hart and replaced by a 'rule theory'. According to a rule theory, law is not comprised of individual commands but of abstract norms which oblige citizens and authorities alike to respect the law (the rule of law), and its basic meaning is identical to the requirement of formal justice that like cases be treated alike. Hart emphasises the 'democratic' element in his theory by subscribing to a positivist theory of law which does not allow any censorship of law on the basis of morals or natural law. According to Hart, a law may be 'immoral' but it cannot be 'invalid' if it was arrived at in accordance with the 'rule of recognition', i.e. social rules for the production of 'valid law'. Hart's theory has been attacked from various sides, but most attacks have been directed not so much at flaws in the theory as at its limited perspective. Lon Fuller's criticism of the 'inner morality' of law (1969) misses the mark insofar as 'inner morality' determines 'function' and not validity, according to his own statement. Hart's 'minimum content of law' is close to Fuller's eight basic functions, and Hart is correct in finding them present in all known legal cultures. Ronald Dworkin's criticism disputes the validity of Hart's contention that the legal system is not exhaustive and that certain unregulated situations leave the judicial decision to the judge's opinion, due, as mentioned, to the limitation of the content of the theory. Hart does not include judicial decisions in his analysis, which is why the problem of the application of law does not affect his view of law.

Hart emphasises the 'internal perspective' of law as essential for the judge or civil servant who is to apply it, and who cannot, therefore, stop at a theory of prognosis ('external perspective') as the lawyer or 'the bad man' can. Those with a responsibility for applying the law must know what they are *obliged* to base their decision on. The judicial decision must *be justified with* arguments which are based on 'valid law' and which will lead to the 'judgment'. It is not sufficient, as American realism did, to understand the judicial decision as a psychological decision causally derived from a virtual *motivational relationship*.

Although Hart subscribes to analytical language philosophy with its recognition of the 'open texture' of language, he still thinks that 'common sense' can lead to a correct description of facts, and he therefore sees no need to distance himself from the objective language theory of logical empiricism, which sees nothing problematic in the linguistic description of legal facts. With the Hermeneutic school's rejection of descriptive objectivity and its recognition of 'intersubjectivity' and consensus in various 'auditoriums' – including that of law – it is clear that both the application and the study of law must take into account descriptions of factual or hypothetical 'legal cases', thus 'qualifying' or 'framing' reality in a system of language concepts and 'interpreting' legal rules on the basis of their language content with regard to purpose and practical effect.

As already mentioned, these observations imply that the process of qualification holds within its compass the cultural situation at large, the social and political reality, including the entire politico-legal system, and the principles of law. It is therefore incorrect for Hart to think that there are 'holes' in law which must be filled in according to the free opinion of the judge, as stated in Section One of the Swiss Statute Book. It is easy to agree with Joseph Raz (1970) that legal systems are formally exhaustive insofar as the judge will always come to a decision because he must. Neither is Dworkin accurate in discriminating between 'rules' and 'directive rules' or in viewing the latter as something separate from law. 'Principles' are either part of the argumentation material, which is allowed within the tradition of legal science *de sententia ferenda* (advice to the courts) and so part of the legal source material, i.e. of law, or they lie outside this material, and arguments based on them become *de lege ferenda* (advice to the legislature).

3. Rule – principle

It has always been known that legal rules must be interpreted, but it is only recently that the principal problems of language philosophy have been recognised, problems which mean that interpretation and application must be seen as a comprehensive 'process of concretisation', as Karl Engisch expressed it as early as 1953. It was this recognition which made me come to regard 'legal principles', 'general guidelines' and 'legal ideas' as necessary parts of the judicial system and the basis of legal argumentation.

Therefore, to look at this theory as a kind of new natural law occupying a middle course between *Begriffsjurisprudenz* and 'legal realism' is neither very interesting nor an original. German legal phenomenology, and the interest theory had already expressed the same purpose, the former referring to intuition, the latter to teleology as the means by which we recognise the rules' underlying values which govern their concretisation. Existentialism also regards legal rules as incomplete drafts for solving problems. These drafts must then be given their final formulation in the individual legal decision, which will then constitute the rule. Certain variants of the system theory, particularly those by N. Luhmann (1969) and Werner Krawietz (1978), who regard law as a social constituent system, continuously adjusting to a complicated social reality, conceal the same decisionist character under a mantel of exhaustiveness. Like existentialist theories, this system theory is related to the Chicago school of market-oriented legal economy theory as developed by R.H. Coase and R. Posner.

The inadequacy of such theories for our understanding of law is evident from the following simplified model: in a park are two lawns, each with a sign. The first sign reads: 'Keep off the grass, penalty for violation £1'. The second sign reads: 'Step on the grass, price £1'. When the money is counted, there will be no difference between the two cases from an economic point of view. From a legal point of view, however, the purpose of the two signs is clearly different.

This model clearly shows that while a sociological, economic and existentialist perspective of law is interesting and relevant, it is not exhaustive, and it fails to distinguish one essential point of practical importance: dogmatics is the study of rights and obligations. General legal theories, which start from and hypostatise the 'reflexive', 'existentialist' or 'market economic' perspectives of law, are an expression of an 'anarchic' ideology which, like the neo-Marxist ideology of the sixties and seventies, imagines a society made up of 'autonomous' groups or individuals.

4. New criticism

The 'new criticism' theories or new 'theories of natural law' also envisage a social development in which minority groups, who lack the opportunity of influencing legislation through parliamentary systems, can use the courts as a tool to reform society by taking out 'promises of future legislation' from con-

stitutional law and introducing arguments based on such
promises in support of claims under administrative law and
civil law. Such a procedure is favoured in a federal system like
that of the United States, where the absence of a common legal
system allows the federal courts considerable 'political' influence
in testing the constitutionality of 'legislation'. There can be no
doubt that the system has been used in this way. We need only
look at the endorsement of Roosevelt's 'New Deal legislation'
and Eisenhower's 'racial integration legislation'. In recent years
the situation has become more acute with the majority decision
of the Supreme Court to reject the death penalty, and its subsequent reintroduction by a new majority.

The same method has also been used with some success in
the Federal Republic of West Germany for the introduction of
legal reforms. Particular reference has been made to the need to
interpret a civil Statutes Book (*BGB*), based on the Nineteenth
Century individualist theory of will, in light of the new Federal
Republic's 'socio-political' constitution (Wiethölter). On the other
hand, the General Clause of 242 *BGB*, which states that the law
must be interpreted with regard to *Treu und Glauben*, has proved
a highly flexible and often adopted adaptation tool, so flexible,
in fact, that it even succeeded in adapting the law to the Nazi
Gesundes Volksempfinden.

For a number of years, critical movements have succeeded
in obtaining results in the courts which they were unable to
achieve through legislative procedures. Particularly in the
United States and the Federal Republic of Germany, where
states and federation have different jurisdictions, the constitution has proved a useful political tool in the courts by
constituting a kind of 'new natural law'. Realising their lack of
a political mandate, however, the courts have recently begun to
take a more restrictive stance.

It has been realised that there are limits to the 'political'
function of the courts and that there is therefore also a distinction between 'legal arguments' (*de sententia ferenda*, i.e.
advice to the court) and 'political arguments' (*de lege ferenda*, i.e.
advice to the legislature). Legal politics is a respectable and
important legal science, but it cannot be hypostasised to 'legal

science'. It is no accident that, like Eastern European socialist law theory, Scandinavian realism placed emphasis on the pedagogical and regulatory effect of law and on public utility as its basic value.

For the working lawyer, valid 'rights and obligations' are the crucial issues, whether his duties are those of a judge who must settle conflicts, a civil servant who must administer, or a lawyer who must negotiate or conciliate, or whether, as a designer of contracts, collective agreements or rules in public administration and private organisations, his task is to prevent conflict. It is characteristic that theorists espousing a 'new liberal' ideology, in opposition to the welfare state's bureaucracy, the justification of which is 'public utility' or 'distributive justice', use the market economy of the social contract to legitimise 'commutative justice' and present the rule of law as a value in competition with public utility. Contrary to Scandinavian realism, which regarded rights and obligations as 'terminological aids', the new liberal theory takes rights seriously.

5. Pre-legal facts: Institutions

a) *Institutional facts*

There is a difference in principle between a 'metalegal' ideology in the name of which rights and obligations are legitimised, and the acknowledgement by legal dogmatics of the existence of valid rules and their derivatives, legal rights and obligations. As explained above, rights and obligations can only be derived from normative conditions and not from facts, unless the fact in question is an 'institutional fact', such as a constituent assembly. Kelsen's *Grundnorm* is a logical precondition for his legal system. Indeed, systems as systems can generally only refer to themselves. Hart's 'rule of recognition' is the empirical fact which every social system approves as its criterion for the production of valid law, whether custom, as in primitive societies, or political practice, as in England, or a constitution which sets a legislative procedure, as in other countries. It is clear that the establishment of this 'institutional fact' cannot be explained in normative terms, but must be classed among the pre-legal facts which law in general is forced to posit.

Every 'social contract' is a hypothetical or fictional entity, the purpose of which is to legitimise the legal system with reference to something rational, namely human reason. It is obvious, on the other hand, that 'legal obligations' established through agreement require that the agreement be binding, and since antiquity, biological-anthropological facts have been recognised as the factual basis of legal and social systems. Aristotle sought the basis of law in man's dual nature as a social and rational being, *zoon politikon*. The later Catholic and material natural law philosophers from Thomas to Grotius also based law on natural facts and man's reasoned will. Hobbes, on the contrary, developed his theory from a more pessimistic view of society, assuming that man is by nature asocial, but the later Anglo-Scottish empiricism is based on the assumption that man's egotistical actions will lead to social gains, thanks to the intervention of an 'invisible hand'. ('Private vices, public benefits', Mandeville, *The Beehive*).

Based on Kant's distinction between nature and obligation, however, F.C. von Savigny (1814) took his starting point in the factually present *Lebensverhältnisse* from which he constructed the corresponding *Rechtsverhältnisse*. Like his Danish contemporary, A.S. Ørsted, Savigny was inspired to take this step by Montesquieu's relative natural law, which required *rapports nécessaire* between the natural conditions of any given society and the legal rules corresponding to them. 'The nature of things' played an important role both for Savigny and Ørsted as a source of legal rules, but while Savigny explained the rules of law as legal manifestations of the 'national genius' (*Volksgeist*), i.e. the sources of Roman law, Ørsted found his inspiration in practical 'factual considerations' (1822). The 'nature of things' and 'case-specific logical structures' have become popular figures in subsequent theories in the argumentation for certain preferred problem solutions. It is clear that, like references to justice and conceptions of justice etc., such arguments have no more value than other evaluative statements and must therefore be supported by clarifying arguments, either with reference to the implied values and purposes, or to the authority of the evaluator. Reality is not 'rationally' structured, which is why it is meaningless to talk of 'case-specific logical structures'.

Neither can a reference to the 'nature of things' alone establish any 'necessary connection' between facts and obligations, although in psychological terms it may exert some normative power (Jellinek 1914).

b) *Nature – culture*

It was the ambition of phenomenology, with the aid of an intuitive insight called *Wesenschau*, to formulate ontological statements on human nature and to derive normative conclusions from this. Kant had wanted to go no further than to deduce, from the principle of individual freedom and responsibility, a right to freedom, limited only by other people's equal right of freedom and by the principle that man is society's goal and not its means. But now things were taken further, and entire ethical and legal systems were deduced on the basis of 'institutional facts'.

It is a correct observation to say that legal rules must be based on man's *biological nature* and *cultural organisation*, but intuition is an ungovernable tool for 'feeling' one's way to the demands of nature. The biological and anthropological sciences are more reliable in spite of the fact that it is difficult to decide what, in present-day social life, is 'nature' and what is 'culture'. One thing is, however, certain: man is of necessity a social being insofar as some degree of division of labour and organisation is needed for the survival of the species. This need arises from the fact that human infants are helpless for several years, mainly because of the size of the brain which enables us to create culture and to adapt to culture in compensation for our poverty of instinct. These 'family institutions' are therefore necessary, just as 'religious institutions' are necessary, provided that the palaeontological criterion for determining human status holds, a criterion which looks for evidence of burial rites as indirect evidence of religious ideas. On the other hand, it is probable that the institution of 'ownership' and 'right of inheritance' are culturally determined, as the original hunter-gatherer cultures were not interested in ownership and family succession. These interests only arose with the emergence of agriculture.

It is generally not easy to establish with any certainty what natural needs are, and even less to say which rules and institutions are required to satisfy them. It is certain, however, that man is not 'an island entire of itself' amenable to statistical handling like natural phenomena and logical entities. Human beings react to natural and legal challenges, turning themselves into players in the legal game and thus limiting the scope for legal regulation. It is also clear that there are limits to the social and cultural conditions to which man can adjust without suffering mental or social wounds in the form of insanity and criminality. But an 'ontological' view of man's 'nature' as such is dangerous, as it leads to intolerance. A political process can, however, be adapted to nature and culture, especially if there is a system in place which will at one and the same time facilitate the communication of human preferences and their long-term arrangement in order of priority.

It is impossible to prove scientifically what form of social organisation may be 'natural' for man, only that some form of social organisation is necessary. There is a good deal of evidence to indicate that the line of development has been from a collective, status-oriented perception of man in primitive societies based on a barter economy to an individualistic and contract-based perception in urban societies with division of labour and a money economy. Reciprocity is the material condition, linking the objective and the subjective techniques for distributing wealth. *Quid pro quo* is the balancing act, serving to unite the propitiating religious sacrifice with commutative justice, the most ancient form of justice, according to Aristotle, and based on proportionality: consideration for promise in the law of contract, and an eye for an eye in the law of sanctions. The objective and material form is gradually replaced by a subjective and formal understanding, according to which the establishing and interpreting of private declarations of intention is the justification and legal effect of both the social and private contract.

With the advent of a more comprehensive social authority,

public utility and *distributive justice* make their appearance as supplements to commutative justice. While modern philosophers have tended to regard distributive justice and the law's regulatory function as the more important aspects, it was, in fact in historical terms, commutative justice and the reflexive, state-oriented understanding of law which was the primary form. This is not to say that the primitive 'communist' society was the original one, although the *hierarchical* element in society developed with the development of the agrarian family society. The word 'hierarchy' implies a divine or holy order, and its basis is precisely a religious notion that something or somebody holds an elevated position. There is no reason, therefore, to believe in the Marxist notion that law will wither away in a communist society based on autonomous decentralised groups. Every modern technological society requires organisation and administration which must become more and more comprehensive as product distribution and markets become more and more international. The nation-state was a fitting framework for the dawn of technology with its need for capital, and a relatively limited market. Imperialism was an attempt, as industry grew, to satisfy the need for raw materials and bigger markets within this romantic framework. Two world wars were the result. Post-war international market organisations are the adequate answer to this development, but they do in turn weaken the regulatory scope of the nation-state, as tax laws and social policies must be adjusted to enable international competition. This is the reason why, at present, we are experiencing a crisis in the 'welfare state's' distributive scope, as the bureaucracy is unwilling and inadequately equipped to watch over 'public utility' in favour of its own interests. With international competition forcing considerations of efficiency upon the nation-states, they are therefore gradually driven to introduce elements borrowed from contract law into their social organisation, thereby allowing individuals to seek to maximise their profits while minimising the cost of transactions.

It is probably true that Kelsen's theory of law will lose most of its relevance in the society of the future, based as it is upon the identification of law and state. It would be wrong, on the other hand to expect a 'neo-socialist' reflexive law based on a belief in the 'withering away of the state' to become a fact of life. Although the importance of the nation-state will decline in the future, an international organisation and bureaucracy will most probably be required for the foreseeable future. Certainly, a life without 'law' would require a level of international prosperity and equalisation which are at best very much in the distant future.

It is, however, possible to formally conclude from what we know of existing human societies that the necessary conditions for an organised form of society must be fulfilled. The minimum conditions must involve communication and function. In order for communication to succeed, a great degree of inter-subjectivity and truth is necessary; and in order for society to function, a minimum of peace and order must be maintained. Hart's 'minimum content' and Fuller's 'inner morality' reflect very well the basic characteristics of the legal orders of known advanced and primitive societies. They also reflect the moral code of the 'Ten Commandments' and K.E. Løgstrup's 'sovereign expressions of life' (1956).

PLURALIST AND RELATIONIST LEGAL SCIENCE

The point of the above analysis is that legal science without legal philosophy has no coherence, that legal philosophy without ideology is without direction, and that ideology without regard to the pre-legal facts is impossible. In other words, if there is to be a meaning in legal science, the science must be anchored in a method which will secure both consistency and substance; there must be connection between the legal scientist's attitude to particular problems and the various areas of law.

There is an essential reciprocity between contemporary science and its interest in, and hence its need for, the questions which science wants to ask – and can ask, and thus also for the methods used and the answers obtained.

Like every language activity, science is a purposeful act and its purpose arises out of certain interests. Every age has its philosophical problems. They stem from the contemporary world picture and way of life and they are solved on the basis of suitable methods. Such problems are defined by the reigning political ideology which express in systematic form the needs and desires which man's biological nature require society to fill under the reigning cultural conditions.

The object of science changes form with the methods and 'measuring equipment' it uses. The 'nature' of law also changes as the methods of legal science change. Law was seen first as an ancient divine custom, then as rules based on agreements with the prince by divine right, then as moral expressions of human reason, then as a system of logical concepts derived from the idea of justice, then as a tool of state control and as a structural module in a complicated social system. Central to the legal sciences at all times is 'dogmatics', the practical legal science, the task of which is always – regardless of the reigning general philosophy – to guide administration and legal practice by making decisions on the question of what constitutes obligatory law.

Like Marxist theory, the sociological and system theories are macro-theories, i.e. theories which approach law from the outside as ideology and behaviour. This is in contrast to *microtheories* which approach the law from within as obligatory norms. System theories regard legal rules as subsidiary in relationship to other social behavioural norms, including ethics. The fact that these theories have become more and more dominant is connected with a growing scepticism regarding the normative power of law in our modern pluralist society, where powerful interest groups combined with generally high educational levels undermine social solidarity and provide avenues for parts of the population to neutralise the effects of heavy administrative regulation. The alternative is to appeal to personal interests, either through 'privatisation' or by creating 'decentralised' systems of government. The weakness of the first choice is less equality, and of the second, less efficiency and concern for the interests of the whole.

The object of Medieval jurisprudence with its dialectic-logical methods was to erect a framework around the contemporary static, or at most slowly-developing, family society, as the inherited status relationships were regulated by custom and authoritative sources of law, *Corpus Iuris* and *Corpus Canonici*.

Renaissance and Age of Enlightenment mechanical-rationalist theory of natural law reflected the absolutist state's use of law as a tool for controlling society without regard to traditional customs, but for the furtherance of the state. the Nineteenth Century's *Begriffsjurisprudenz* with its attempt at honing an organic system of legal concepts was intended as a tool for the expanding technology within the nation-state and private capitalism.

During the Eighteenth Century rationalism and the Nineteenth Century idealism, science was guided by the same kind of rationalism. Thought was put first and projected on to the external world, which was assumed to be structured in terms of language. Around the turn of the century this rationalism was rejected and replaced by various types of irrationalism and realism. Both schools acknowledged that the principal difficulty was to combine thought and reality, and especially cognition and evaluation.

American pragmatism in fact gave up seeking an objective criterion for truth, as both theoretical and practical knowledge were guided by expediency, and scientific knowledge by consensus among scientists. Within the legal sciences this situation gave rise to sociological and pragmatic schools patterned on behaviourist social and psychological models of adaptation and prognosis. Continental 'intuitionism' first spawned a 'sociological' *Freirecht* theory, and later a teleological interest theory.

By separating law and reality completely, the later Vienna school and Kelsen's 'pure theory of law' attempted to protect law against ideological and political control, but instead propagated a pure form of that reduction of law, begun by *Begriffsjurisprudenz*, to a tool for state control of society, now also including civil law. The so-called Scandinavian realism also saw law as a state tool for changing society and for the internalisation of behavioural norms. Marxist regimes in the west and communist regimes in the east with their totalitarian ideologies also saw legal rules as the means for achieving rapid social change, placing major emphasis on both pedagogical and authoritarian methods, in that both propaganda and the threat of force were important elements.

With its principles of positivism and objective concepts of duty, the English analytical theory also accentuated the role of law as a tool for social control, but it revealed a less authoritarian attitude by emphasising the abstract nature of rules of law contrary to the continental and Scandinavian command theory.

The showdown with the view of law as a technical tool of state control marked the post-war new natural law theories and system theories. The new natural law theories appealed in various ways for the introduction of 'extra-judicial' principles to act as a moral check on the content of law, and thus of the way society was organised. System theories have appealed particularly for various procedures for the securing of certain values. Some of these procedures fall back on 'communication', 'rhetorics' and 'dialectics', trusting in the ability of human reason to control social developments (Habermas 1968, Perelman 1963). Others place emphasis on the structure of the system as the means of securing 'fairness' (Rawls 1971, Dworkin 1986), and still others refer to 'market economy' and other impersonal mechanisms, arguing that legal rules continuously adapt themselves to other social processes (Luhmann 1969, Teubner 1983).

We have seen that the various theories of law, both past and present, rest on a political ideology. We have also seen that the revolt against Nineteenth Century idealism and rationalism took various forms. New natural law theories express an idealist epistemology in that they believe that we create our social surroundings by mentally projecting our values on to them, while system theories, on the other hand, deny the normative character of the law. A theory of law which sees pre-legal facts, i.e. 'natural' and 'cultural' facts, as 'institutional facts', and their inherent values as necessary constituents of the language in which legal rules are expressed and in which reality must be described, does not have the same epistemological difficulties. A philosophy of law based on historical, comparative and social facts will become a 'social theory' which constructs hypotheses to be confirmed or dismissed through the political process. A theory of law which regards law as 'obligations' to be considered from different angles will be relationist and not relativist. It follows that legal dogmatics must be realist, but not in the form of 'unprincipled realism'.

Individual legal institutions must be seen as part of a whole, and individual legal rules must be understood in light of the entire legal and cultural system's underlying purposes, and in solving concrete and hypothetical questions of law, it is necessary to interpret the rule and describe facts in such a way that the decision reached will achieve such legal effects as are compatible with law and order and the purpose of the rule. Like every language expression, every rule is intentional and teleological. In legal decisions, the task is to realise this purpose and, through a choice between the possible alternative interpretations, to achieve the 'correct' legal effects (pragmatism).

No action can be purposive unless it has a purpose. Neither

can 'real considerations' point in a direction if the goal is un-known. Arguments of this character are just as empty as idealist references to 'justice', no more in fact than erratic expressions of individual values. A realist stance adopted on principle must therefore openly consider the rule's presumed goal and the choice of possible legal effects made available by language interpretation.

Such a combination and systematic ordering of factual, ideo-logical, philosophical and dogmatic elements is necessary in a science of law which is coherent and focused on reality: a pluralist and relationist legal science.

I second Kierkegaard's dilemma, that we must live our lives *forwards*, while only being able to understand and explain our actions *backwards*.

In youth we are obliged to act, although we do not have the experience of age and therefore do not always know what we are doing or why we do it. This is both necessary and valuable because otherwise we could make no progress.

I shall end by repeating the words of Johann Gottlieb Fichte from the early Nineteenth Century, one of the first to under-stand the relative and purposive nature of cognition:

Was für eine Philosophie man wähle hängt davon ab, was man für ein Mensch ist, denn ein philosophisches System ist beseelt durch die Seele des Menschen, der es hat.

Although no-one today would subscribe to Fichte's subjective idealism, which leaves it to the individual to create his own universe by projecting his ideas on to an unstructured sur-rounding world, it is more reassuring than Hegel's objective idealism, which sees the individual as a passive tool for the march of reason down through history and as a tiny wheel in the huge machinery of the state.

Today this clash is being repeated. After the collapse of logical empiricism and the belief in 'objective' knowledge, the link between cognition and consciousness has again come into focus. In order to avoid landing in 'anarchistic' subjectivism, which makes any organised society an impossibility, various paths were explored for the construction of an 'inter-subjective' understanding. Language, our only tool of scientific knowledge, must contain such inter-subjective elements if it is to serve as a medium of communication. According to this view, language is a necessary tool for the organisation of society, without which the human species cannot survive.

Language capacity and consciousness belong together and are the counterparts of an extreme lack of instinct which makes it possible for human beings to adapt to such changes in social conditions which the human consciousness is capable of creating. On the one hand, language, not least writing, is capable of retaining the past as a feeling of identity, but also of preserving it in the form of 'history', given that experience is the basis of recognition and understanding. The new rhetoric with its various 'auditoriums' faced backwards and took a historical perspective in its consensus criterion. Heidegger also spoke of *Vorverständnis* and *intentionality* as conditions for knowledge.

A knowledge of the past and our motives is decisive for exercising that choice among various possibilities, which is identical with 'being' (living). According to Heidegger, the choice is not free, but limited to the possibilities available in any given situation. A person who asks about the nature of things has already assumed that it is possible to talk scientifically on this subject. Such an ontological standpoint can easily lead to a superior attitude which can extend to include totalitarian ideologies.

The 'liberating' ideology emphasises the creative possibilities of language, either by stressing the 'rational dialogue', like Habermas, or, like pragmatism, by accepting human feelings and interests as part of the momentum in social processes.

Pluralist philosophy is tied to pluralist ideology and sharpens the awareness of a pluralist (relationist) science in general, and legal science in particular.

TOOLS AND METHODS IN THE SCIENCE OF LAW

1. History and function

The study of law has followed two paths through the centuries. One of them sees legal science purely as the task of interpreting authoritative texts. The second takes its starting point in the 'facts of the matter', assuming that there is a 'necessary connection' between norm and reality: that reality is logically constituted, so to speak.

The former method was that employed by the early Romanists in Bologna in the Eleventh Century. Their work was based on *Corpus Iuris* which, like other works from Greek and Roman antiquity, was considered an authoritative text, and on the view that their task was to perform a dogmatic exegesis of this text in the same manner in which contemporary theologians were interpreting the Bible and canonical writings. Commenting or glossing the text in the margin, the glossators resolved contradictions through *distinctiones* and filled in vacuums by analogy in order to systematise their facts in accordance with traditional rhetorical scholarship.

The conceptual structure had been developed in the Hellenistic (late classical) Greek philosophy in continuation of Aristotle's theory of logic. Its aim was, through definition and analysis of concepts, to establish a fundamental genus- and species-related basis on which irrefutable conclusions (*syllogisms*) could be drawn, thus building eternal truth from changeable facts. The Renaissance goal was to revive classical (Greek) methods of scholarship, but Renaissance scholars applied these methods to the old Greek texts which they considered authoritative. This school of thought was known as *more geometrico* or *more italicus* and, to sum up, it adopted the systematic, authoritative and logical method of Scholastic and canonical scholarship, the ideal of which was the certainty of the results obtained by the method.

Catholic ethics and the later rationalist natural law of the Seventeenth and Eighteenth Centuries preserved fundamentally the same link to the mathematical sciences, but after the Copernican revolution in cosmology it sought its ideal in physics and mechanics, presenting legal science arguments as cause and effect relations, although still based on doctrine and not on facts (maxims from which legal relations followed). They thus sought the cause of the rule of law and not its explanation.

The idea of an eternal and immutable natural law which human reason was able to comprehend collapsed in the late 1700s. Hume's and Kant's critiques introduced the fundamental distinction between the *realm of necessity*, i.e. the external world which we must presume to be governed by causation, although we cannot prove it, and the *realm of freedom*, i.e. the world of ethics and law and free will, the existence of which is equally beyond proof, but which must be presumed to exist as the concept of responsibility would otherwise be rendered meaningless. It is therefore impossible to arrive at valuation from knowledge, from 'is' to 'ought', from 'sein' to 'sollen'.

In the meantime, in his greatest work *The Spirit of the Laws*, Montesquieu had rejected the idea of an absolute law of nature, while replacing it with the idea of a relative law of nature founded on a *rapport necessaire* between social conditions and legal requirements. 'Nature des choses' was the term used for this by Montesquieu himself. A.S. Ørsted was later to base his *Håndbog* and his development of Danish jurisprudence on Montesquieu's metaphysics. *Forholdets natur* was the key concept used by Ørsted to fill out the legal vacuum which had arisen in the 200 year history of Danish law.

Around the turn of the century, it became clear that no such *rapport necessaire* existed, as reality is not a product of the human mind (subjective idealism, Fichte), neither is reality inherently logical (objective idealism, Hegel). In common with the British and Scandinavian analytical schools, later 'logical empirical' epistemologies and schools of ethics presumed that it was possible to describe the external world in an objective (mathematical) language, and they repeated the criticism of the 'naturalist fallacy', which consisted of drawing normative conclusions from ordinary events. Hans Kelsen and his Danish student Alf Ross maintained that one cannot arrive at 'ought' from 'is', and that science should therefore be concerned only with 'reality', but that it is, on the other hand, possible to describe reality in objective terms. Otherwise it would not be possible to 'verify' a claim concerning the facts of a case or to limit science to logical statements (analytical sentences) or to statements about reality (synthetic sentences). Metaphysical and evaluative statements were, on the other hand, unscientific. One cannot meaningfully speak of angels and justice because such statements are incapable of verification.

This analytical and empirical theory of law was thus reduced to the task of 'describing' existing rules and to using ordinary logical systematic methods for this description, which, on the other hand, would allow conclusions to be drawn with certainty and with no evaluative (moral) elements superimposed. Another possibility was, according to American realism, to calculate the judge's hypothetical decision in advance and use this calculation as basis for one's views, a result of the pragmatic epistemology ('what is right is what is successful'). Alf Ross attempted to unite this pragmatism with the socio-psychological theory of law (Hägerström 1908, Olivecrona 1939), which, based on the concept of the 'common good', saw law as the feeling of being bound by an 'independent imperative'.

The welfare state's social democratic fathers in Sweden and Denmark saw the law and the state as two sides of the same coin and the law as the instrument available to the altruistic state in deciding the 'good life' for its citizens. Rules of law were therefore no longer seen as a means of guaranteeing individual rights in dealings with the state, but as tools for creating welfare. Suitability therefore became a key concept in jurisprudence, the purpose of which was to realise intentions which could be derived from the rules of law and related legislative materials.

In the 60s, this logical-positivist science came under criticism from hermeneutic and 'critical' theories, claiming that it was false and suppressive respectively. The hermeneutic school took a radical approach, attacking the supposition regarding language objectivity and the possibility of strict separation of 'knowledge' and 'evaluation'. Language is not a property of things, but a tool used in communication. One therefore cannot assume that things have names: quite the contrary. Names must be given on the basis of subjective and inter-subjective evaluations, and such evaluations must necessarily be inter-subjective if language is to serve as a means of communication.

The consequences of this Hermeneutic language theory are that it forces the legal sciences to adopt an entirely different approach to law than they have traditionally done. If legal rules are norms, they must be approached as part of the general culture, i.e. as part of a society's fundamental basic values, whether such rules take the form of medieval customs or modern laws. In order to understand and interpret our political system with its concomitant, political democracy, we must understand the result of the development of European individualism, which sees people as sovereign beings, society's end and not its means, i.e. beings with rights which may be defended by independent courts. The rights of the individual must, however, be regulated to allow room for other human beings' similar rights. The ranking required to achieve this balance can only be decided by the state, which must effect its purpose through legislation and gradually, as its gains ground, begin to exercise 'distributive' justice (welfare) in supplement to 'commutative' justice (equality before the law, *isonomy*).

The law governing legal capacity, family and inheritance is based on the principles of liberty and sovereignty, while property law must consider trade and circulation interests. This is why the doctrine of will or intentions finds itself in competition with the doctrine of objective interpretation in the law of contract and property, not least within business law, where quick decisions are required on the basis of recognisable external facts. In contrast, public law must accord a higher ranking to general public interests and the interest of authority, but must not forget to weigh these interests against the concern for the rule of law and the administration of the law. More recently, with the development of the welfare state into a 'high tax society', the interests of the welfare state have been forced into a less prominent role. The legislative materials, and hence the subjective teleological interpretation, give way to the objective purposeful construction, according to which the letter of the law is valid law.

The principle of justice is particularly dominant in criminal law, where the protection of individual rights makes it incumbent on society to prove that the accused is guilty of a crime under the law (*nullum crimen sine lege*). Procedural rules aim in general to ensure that the burdens of presumption and of proof are placed on those parties who have the opportunity and encouragement to secure themselves. Bankruptcy and insolvency rules serve the same purpose: to guarantee equal distribution of the risk of financial collapse unless individual persons have been granted a security interest in return for establishing a credit facility.

When we interpret and apply the law, our foundation must always be the authoritative materials, the laws, their derivations, customs and contracts. We must apply a Hermeneutic epistemology and language theory, a democratic social theory and a teleological pragmatic theory of law. We must keep in mind that legal science has attempted through centuries to establish certain and predictable legal decisions through *rules of construction* aimed at strengthening the *rule of law*. Not enough attention has been given to the fact, however, that the *description* of legal facts is a dialectic process which partly selects facts on the basis of the rule to be applied, and partly describes the rule in light of the pragmatic interests affected by the legal consequences inherent in the decision. Neither the construction of the rules nor the description of facts is an objective deduction, but a legal *decision* which, in the final analysis, it must be possible to express in the form of a language syllogism consisting of a major premise (the defining rule), a minor premise (the qualifying legal fact) and the logical inference: IT IS HELD THAT.

The study of law and the application of law thus employ the same pluralist hermeneutic tool, which requires an understanding of the fundamental values on which the legal system and the relevant section of the law is based. Without *telos* (purpose), no teleology. The purpose of law rules is not merely to be used for interpreting a legal text as one would interpret a literary text, where the focus may be placed on either the sender's or the recipient's purpose. The law must be approached as a normative instrument of control aimed at influencing a social reality in a particular political direction. When assessing facts, whether actual or hypothetical, it is necessary to weigh the various possible descriptions in light of one's knowledge of the relevant social conditions, in order to assess what practical consequences the application of the rule would have relative to its practical object. This ranking of the various practical considerations in light of the rule's purpose presumes a professional judgment which experience shows can only be exercised by lawyers, as technicians and other professions (doctors, architects, engineers) are prone to perform a more pedantic and language-based construction. Lawyers have known since classical antiquity that commutative and distributive justice must also compete with equity (*epieikeia*), a necessity caused by the difficulty of applying general rules to specific situations.

The study of law is thus not exclusively a descriptive-interpretative activity, but has also a *creative* element, the purpose of which is a never-ending process of adapting the rules of law handed down to us by former generations to the ever-changing social conditions. In this light, to identify connections in the legal source materials capable of contributing to the work of related sciences and to resolve, in this context, (apparent) contradictions through analysis and distinction. Also, through analogous and contradictory inferences involving other parts of the system, to create harmony, and thus to adapt the law to reality and to maintain and increase the level of harmony in the legal system.

2. Empiricism, rationalism and the computer in science

a) *Theory*

The word empiricism derives from the Greek *'pirein'*, which means to learn by observation and experiment. This is what the Greeks did, in contrast to all earlier cultures. They observed nature and their own society in order to find (*metodos*: 'the road by which ...') 'the infinite in the finite'. The Greeks had learnt much from the earlier Babylonian and Phoenician cultures, whose work had, however, been limited to recording and cataloguing. Like the Egyptians, the Babylonians were an agricultural civilisation, dependent on the seasons and the weather for the flooding and irrigation of fields, while the Phoenicians, being seafarers and traders, were interested in the practical application of their experience.

The alphabet developed by the Phoenicians was based on the pictogram and the cuneiform writing systems which had developed in Egypt and Mesopotamia, but it stood out by its quality of perfect abstraction, achieved by dividing the words into distinct sounds written as a string of letters which could be combined into an infinite number of words. Like all other Semitic alphabets, the Phoenician alphabet had no vowels. These were introduced by the Greeks in order to create a perfect sound representation, which in turn promoted the analytical ability, at the same time as Greek, being an Indo-European language, distinguished between subject and object. It goes without saying that such a purpose-oriented language, combined with a writing system composed of characters, promotes conceptualisation with regard to cause and effect, technology and politics.

Analysis and synthesis are Greek concepts, where analysis refers to the separation of experience into its constituent parts and synthesis to the combination of elements into hypothetical or real relationships. System is a third Greek word for this synthesis of elements in a relationship established according to a theory of the real or ideal world. Empiricism thus implies a process of gathering facts and ordering them according to a hypothetical relationship assumed to exist within the system selected, the ordering process being governed by a set of accepted general values or logical presumptions according to type and example, *genus* and *species*, as Aristotle was later to label them. By using these fundamental concepts, the empiricist was able to draw logical conclusions after having clearly defined (delimited) his concepts.

If we define our concepts on an incomplete experiential basis, we risk defining away important phenomena and properties, thus rendering our 'scientific' inferences incomplete or erroneous. Basic suppositions and theories are not formed through rational or logical operations but through a process which Aristotle called *nous* (intuition), which is a distinct method of thinking, akin to poetic creation. The word derives from the Greek *'theori'* which means to 'observe', and it later developed to mean also the thoughts and impressions which the observation of phenomena awoke within the observer, and again, scientific theories and theorems. Aristotle was not alone in his view that aesthetic considerations are essential elements in the formation of theories. More recently Albert Einstein has made the same point. Simplicity, harmony and universality are the most important aesthetic values involved. The system tolerates no holes or contradictions, and the primary object of science is therefore to fill in holes through analogy and to remove contradictions through analysis and distinctions.

b) *The computer or an empirical-intuitive method*

The more empirical data collected before the theory is formulated, the smaller the risk becomes that one's field of vision is circumscribed and important elements rejected in the process of definition. One cannot, of course, collect data without having a loose theory about their relationship, as the information gathered would otherwise be far too incidental and scattered to yield any meaning. The meaning of the word 'science' is precisely the gathering and sorting of knowledge in accordance with a systematic relationship.

This general interest in knowledge is continuously brought into confrontation with the data gathered *insofar as* the sorting of the material according to a more systematic manner is put off as long as possible, *so as to prevent* the early choice of theory from placing restraints on any further research, *as* the data which do not fit into the theory will be overlooked, because one is looking for something else.

This is why the classical method before the computer age had a greater level of certainty to offer the scientist wanting to avoid this circumscription of his perspective, because the physical materials, such as filing cards, books and notes, could always be arranged according to some new order and links, thus allowing the scientist to maintain a steady overview of large materials while adjusting it according to new patterns based on intuitively felt relationships. The computer image is unambiguous and cannot be split into a multiplicity of simultaneous images, but only into sequences which do not allow the same visual experience of similarities and differences.

The transition to the typewriter created the same dilemma, albeit on a smaller scale, as it was more complicated to correct a piece of writing once typing had begun. The method of production assumed a certain element of control once typing had commenced, in contrast to handwriting, which was more readily changed and corrected, although in principle the same problem existed there.

This hermeneutic problem of the relationship between part and whole is inevitable, but the worst problems can be avoided by putting off the choice of systematics (and hence method) for as long as possible and by using a technology which is not based exclusively on serial material collection and processing. Computer technology contains a risk of unwittingly adopting such a 'serial' method, the problem of which is similar to that of archaeology, where layer is imposed upon layer, excluding the possibility of performing ongoing adjustments as new data are collected in the usual manner.

The deductive/systematic method, on the other hand, proceeds from the initial preparation of a 'synopsis' or systematics based on a set of traditional or intuitively assumed relationships, extrapolated from a hypothetical set of fundamental values. Work which follows this method will be limited to the hypothetical (traditional or intuitive) values and will not be repeatedly assessed in light of new data of a kind which is incompatible with the fundamental values. The work will be governed in a general sense by its 'fundamental value', whether religious, rationalist or idealist. Human 'reason', which is an essential and defining property of man, has governed scientific method since antiquity (Aristotle), through the Middle Ages (Thomas Aquinas) and rationalism (Grotius, Pufendorf 1672), driven by the fundamental assumption that matter has some 'essential' qualities which we must learn to understand. Reason has therefore occupied the top rung of the hierarchy of values which constitute the system derived from this assumption. The so-called *Begriffsjurisprudenz* (1800s) is a continuation of this method, and rather than relativising and adjusting the value system, it expands and narrows its concepts in order to slot in new experiences. If computer programs and models are taken to be expressions of reality and are applied to this reality without adjustment of the programs and models, the application of modern computer technology contains the risk of repeating this fallacy. Like fire, the computer is a good servant but a bad master.

c) *Hermeneutics and theory*

The word hermeneutics derives from 'Hermes', the name of the Greek god who was messenger to the gods, and it refers to the Sophist recognition of the difference or dialectics existing between the letters of words and the meaning of words. To the primitive consciousness, the meaning of words is objective, and the words must be pronounced in a strictly literal way if they are to have the desired effect. Original Roman law and procedural law had this magic and ritual quality, depending for their effect on compliance with the precise forms. Originally oral, the law preserved its strictly formal quality after writing had assumed an important role. It was only in the Second Century BC that the Greek hermeneutic distinction between word and meaning penetrated into the law, where it culminated in Cicero's stoic-rhetoric interpretation theory.

This basic distinction between the spirit and the letter was the leaven of western philosophy from Grotius's contract and political theory of the Sixteenth Century. It continued to make itself felt in the rationalist natural law theory (Pufendorf) and in the idealist theory of the will which, based on the concept of freedom, stressed the importance of the will as the legal grounds on which promises were given and as the criterion determining the scope (interpretation) and limitation (invalidity) of a promise. With reference to the protection of trade and the promisee's 'good faith', the Scandinavian promises and expectations theorists of the mid-Nineteenth Century stressed the general meaning of words and people's expectations of promises received as the criterion of interpretation and validity.

The 'hermeneutic' circle is the paradox arising from the fact that single elements provide no meaning unless the whole is known, and the whole provides no meaning without a knowledge of its parts. Knowledge is therefore by necessity the result of a dialectic process developing in our consideration of the empirical facts on the one hand, and on the other, the theory, which is an expression of the epistemological interest (the purpose). Science has not only a practical, but also a theoretical aim in its gathering of knowledge, namely through the systematic collection of facts to attain generalisations which will facilitate new technological changes of reality and the creation of a new reality (pragmatism). Laws are such technological tools which may be used to work changes in the social reality in step with changes in the external world. The task of legal science is, by its analysis of the interplay between reality and inherited and valid law, to increase our understanding of this interplay.

d) *Conclusion*

It is clear from what has been said above on the topic of 'theory' and systematics that the empirical branch of the legal sciences must seek to attain as comprehensive a knowledge of the legal and social materials as possible so as to allow 'theory' (observation) the broadest possible framework, and so that the further process may consist in a continuous dialectic between empiricism and theory ending in a final conclusion which also expresses the ultimate theory.

One must therefore be aware of the problems in using computers and other technology, for although they multiply the speed and volume of a literature search, they also limit the scope of 'observation' by limiting the scope for simultaneous and dialectic treatment of the (entire) material, thus ultimately limiting the scope for the formation of a meaningful theory.

As I said before, the computer is a good servant but a dangerous master.

GADAMER'S UNIVERSAL HERMENEUTICS

Interpretation has always been lawyers' most important task. In contrast to humanists and aestheticists, lawyers and theologians have a common object, and hence a related method, namely normative texts and a dogmatic exegesis.

When the message is interpreted, it is the sender and not the receiver who takes pride of place. The normative element in authoritative texts necessarily implies a 'right' interpretation which exists independently of the receiver's understanding of it.

The message, the intention, is therefore an important element in the theological and the legal interpretation, and so is the practical element. According to Hans-Georg Gadamer (1965), the difficulty in applying legal rules to concrete events is a core issue of universal Hermeneutics.

Early Hermeneutics pointed out that the historical element is important to the 'understanding' of a text, but the historical horizon was broadened by Heidegger, to whom understanding was man's primary and unavoidable tool for accommodating himself within and relating to the world (and not just to a text or a source which is incomprehensible on a first reading). The historical, contextual element cannot, therefore, be eliminated either from the text or from the interpreter. On the contrary, it creates the *raison d'être* of every act of textual interpretation. Gadamer's contribution is that he saw the significance of the relationship between text and reality in the concretisation of language in practical situations.

Gadamer first published this insight in 1960 in his *Wahrheit und Methode*, and further developed it in his preface and epilogue to the second edition of 1965. The subject of his 'universal hermeneutics' is the relationship between language and reality and the nature and limits of knowledge – a theory which is not just an interpretation of texts but an ontology.

In this Chapter, I shall sketch the contribution of the hermeneutic-rhetorical tradition to the formation of legal theory up to its current influence exerted through Gadamer's universal hermeneutics. Today, we can refer to several recent legal theories which show hermeneutic elements which may or may not be the direct result of Gadamer's work.

1. The theory of law

It is hardly surprising that the development of hermeneutic theory has been the work mainly of legal historians and especially German legal historians; but German, post-war legal dogmatism also sought inspiration in universal hermeneutics. The three most important representatives of this latter hermeneutic theory are Helmut Coing, the first director of the Max-Planck-Institute of European Legal History, Joseph Esser, one of the most influential civil law lawyers of the post-war period and, like Coing, a prominent representative of comparative jurisprudence, and finally Franz Wieacker, civil law historian and specialist in Roman law and dogmatics (1967).

A common feature of these three jurists, however, is the fact that their theories were not derived from Gadamer, but the result of parallel development. Relying in part on Dilthey's older hermeneutics (1833-1911), they treated hermeneutic theory as an extension of rhetoric. Deeply rooted in antiquity, rhetoric developed in the medieval period into one of the most important sources for scholasticism, the science which undertook to harmonise the authoritative classical texts from science, religion, and law.

Contemporary jurisprudence has accepted the necessity of a scientific theoretical foundation on which to build its dogmatic and interpretative theory. As early as the mid-1960's, jurisprudence had given up its empirical-analytical stance and recognised hermeneutics or critical theory as its foundation. Having admitted the impossibility of an objective description of reality, as reality belonged to a different logical category than language, lawyers were no longer satisfied with asking the question: *How*? They also asked: *Why*?

In opposition to the systematic and deductive approach which dominated the Twentieth Century's idealism, jurisprudence currently emphasises the topical rhetorical theory and the open-ended nature of law. The rhetorical dialectical element in legal usage having previously been recognised in the works of Chaim Perelman (1963), Theodor Viehweg (1965) and Stephan Toulmin (1950), Karl Engisch (1968) and Karl Larenz (1979), have focused attention on the discretionary element in the application of law. This element arises from the dialectic between the concrete and the universal in the concept of type. In contrast to the universal concept, the concept of type emphasises the open-ended nature of the undefined concept, a concept which is not constituted by its structure, but by its intensity: What is a forest? How many trees does it take to make one?

The theory of science debate in the 1960s sparked by the positivistic criticism was led among others by Jürgen Habermas (1968). In *Law and Society* (1970), I myself collected the results of my earlier articles into a hermeneutic functionalist theory of law, stressing the intentional nature of knowledge and the necessity of an ideological and anthropological approach to the understanding and interpretation of norms which have an abstract purpose and which are made concrete through pragmatic considerations.

Jørgen Dalberg-Larsen (1977) refers to the points of similarity between the German hermeneutics and the more recent English analytical jurisprudence which, like hermeneutics, emphasises the 'internal' (understanding) element in the concept of law and the creative element in language. Based on Wittgenstein's later work, the Finnish Aulis Aarnio and the Polish-Swedish Aleksander Peczenik have tied themselves to a hermeneutical analytical theory in close co-operation with the Scot, Neil MacCormick.

In order to understand the current interest in hermeneutics within the theory of law and its doctrinal method, we must refer back to the emergence of legal doctrine in ancient Rome. This is the point where, thanks to Roman receptiveness towards the Greek contribution (Aristotle), the awareness first dawned that the authority of the law or the text could be preserved only if it was interpreted, that is to say actualised with respect to a concrete case or a concrete political situation. Rhetoric entered the scene.

2. Rhetoric and jurisprudence

In the oldest Roman procedural law during the time of the Law of the Twelve Tables (ca. 450 BC) there was complete agreement between words and their meaning. The formulas which were the foundation of the procedure would be said strictly according to rituals in order to procure the desired results. If one of the parties failed to provide evidence that once and for all answered the assertion, then the case was dismissed.

This belief in the ritual meaning of words is a familiar feature from folk tales where, like an 'Open Sesame', the magical spell of a single word can open sealed doors or make brooms start and finish work. This magical power inherent in the content of a word is later transferred to writing, where the magic is preserved. We see this in the runes bricked up in the foundations of some of our oldest churches.

The Roman culture preserved these ritualised forms of procedure well into the classical period (from circa 200 BC), albeit in an altered form. At this time, however, Greek culture began to manifest itself in the new schism between *verba* and *voluntas*. In the interpretation of contracts and evidence, the wording was no longer strictly conclusive; rather, it was the meaning which became the interpreter's aim. During the following period, Roman law also adopted the Greek ideal *aequitas* as a general control of reasonableness in the interpretation and application of legal rules. Similarly, *actiones in factum* and *bona fide* became tools for the *praetors'* development of the old strict legal claims and their literal content.

The distinction between word and meaning was first introduced by the Greek sophists, who founded etymology, the study of the meaning of words as part of their dialectic exercises. They were also responsible for introducing the distinction between a universal problem and an individual case, between essential and unessential elements, between word and intention. The sophists carried their subjectivism so far that they were accused of immorality and manipulation. They dismissed all religious moralist conceptions (the gods did not create man, man created the gods; law and society are not ruled by the gods, but by people themselves through a social contract). Plato tells us that Socrates was known for attacking the sophists' ambiguous way of avoiding fixed definitions and arguing from a subjective moral. Plato's and Aristotle's work can be understood as an attempt to find criteria for as broadly objective a knowledge as possible. Plato was, for example, forced to accept Gorgias' teachings on fairness, *epieikeia* – a concept which was to play a key role in legal usage in later periods. In two of his writings on logic, *analytika priora* or the First Analysis, and *analytika posteriora* or the Second Analysis, later collected under the name of *Organon*, Aristotle created the distinction between the correct logical conclusion or syllogism on the one hand and, on the other, the scientific evidence and the principles by which it is established, such as the validity of the first concepts or statements which enter into the premise of a syllogism. Only by a process of abstraction can empirical facts be assigned to language concepts, and only 'catalogues of the most accepted meanings' can be employed in dialectical and rhetorical arguments. While the object of dialectics is to convince, the object of rhetoric is to persuade an audience; their common ground is the topic, which Aristotle discusses in the second part of *Organon*.

In his works on the art of speaking, *De oratore* and *Topica*, Cicero based his summary of classical rhetoric partly on Aristotle's analysis and partly on that of a contemporary of Aristotle, Anaximenes, who wrote the first systematic textbook on rhetoric, a major source in Gaius' textbook on Roman civil law (*Institutiones*, ca. AD 150). Having been incorporated into Justinian's *Corpus Juris* (529-34), this textbook was to become highly influential in later Romanist jurisprudence (the glossators, from around AD 1000).

Like contemporary theologians, the glossators adopted the views and aims of scholasticism, which assumed the authority of the classical sources, including *Corpus Juris*. The object of the glossators was, therefore, to create an unambiguous and exhaustive system on the basis of the scattered and casuistic source materials which had been created over several centuries and which had been valid in a very different age. The *trivium*, the study of grammar, rhetoric and dialectics became the most important tool in this process of harmonisation through *distinctio* and *divisio*. The starting point was a philological exposition, supplemented by an interpretation of the text's *ratio*, its objective intention. Supplementary rules of interpretation were formulated to account for differences on the same or different levels, and the figure of analogy, as well as conclusions *a contrario* and *a fortiori*, were introduced as means to obtain harmony. To account for contradictions between different legal sources, other rules of harmonisation were formulated: *lex posterior derogat priori*, *lex specialis derogat generali*, etc. A number of interpretative viewpoints: systematic, historical, sociological, and ethical, were added later.

Systematic considerations rested on an assumption of textual unity, a basic principle in rhetoric. The historical viewpoint concerned the law's rational meaning, its *ratio*, which was the interpreter's object. Later in the Fourteenth and Fifteenth Centuries, however, the post-glossators began to identify an additional objective in the task of adjusting inherited legal materials to an altered reality, and that is why ethical, sociological and pragmatic factors were introduced into interpretative doctrine.

In the Seventeenth Century, Hugo Grotius accepted the Medieval interpretation theory based on Cicero, passing it on to the historical school through Hume's and Kant's critiques, which had removed the foundation from under objective reason and thus made room for a radical legal positivism. It was not, however, until the introduction of the so-called interest jurisprudence around the mid-Nineteenth Century that sociological viewpoints came to the fore.

Rudolph von Ihering (1872) settled the score with the previous period's idealist *Begriffsjurisprudenz*, perceiving legal rules to be the result of a struggle between political interests and purpose as the guiding principle in interpretation. As Schopenhauer and Nietzsche before him, he saw motive as being the impetus behind human behaviour: *Eine Handlung ohne Motiv ist wie eine Wirkung ohne Ursache.* Ihering's teleological theory, which was strongly influenced by Bentham's utilitarianism, became a major source of inspiration for future jurisprudence, giving rise to a 'sociological *Freirecht* school of thought', the hallmark of which was its determination, which it shared with the existentialists, to assess every specific case on its own terms; and to a school of 'interest jurisprudence', which wanted to hold fast to legislation as the guarantee of due process, but wanted to base interpretation of the law on its objective purpose (teleological interpretation).

3. Hermeneutics and jurisprudence

In sum, jurisprudence was the offspring of rhetoric rather than hermeneutics, although considerable agreement exists between the methods of rhetorical-juridical interpretation and universal hermeneutics. Thus textual autonomy and unity in hermeneutics correspond to the systematic viewpoint in rhetoric (genus/species relationship). The genetic interpretation in hermeneutics (the objective and the subjective purpose) corresponds to the historical teleological viewpoint of rhetoric. The technical interpretation in hermeneutics corresponds to the sociological viewpoint of rhetoric (the relationship between language and reality).

Another common feature is the stress on the comparative element and the topical element in interpretation: no definite rules for ranking the different interpretative viewpoints exist, making interpretation an 'art' rather than a science. Legal interpretation theory was, nevertheless, inspired by rhetoric rather than by hermeneutics until recently.

Only in the 1960s, when hermeneutics had been developed by Heidegger and Gadamer from being a theory of text interpretation into an ontology and general theory of science, did it begin to play an independent role for jurisprudence in Germany and Denmark. The relationship between language and reality became an important theme in the critical theoretical debate with the realisation that empirical-analytical positivism was wrong in its assumption that an impartial, objective description of empirical and legal matters could be achieved.

In Denmark, the legal positivist criticism naturally begins with Alf Ross' realist theory of law, which builds on the thesis, deriving from logical empiricism, that science consists of statements with 'semantic reference' and that there is a process of verification which can determine objectively whether the statement is true or false. The theory rests on the assumption, of course, that it is possible to describe the external world in objective terms, implying by its formulation that evaluations are unscientific.

This, however, is exactly the point which the hermeneutical theory stresses: *that* all concepts are intentional, *that*, as the hermeneutical circle demonstrates, we cannot understand a part of the whole without knowing the whole and its meaning and *that* we cannot grasp the whole without knowing its fractional elements, and finally *that* our mental horizon, circumscribed as it is by our historical and social context, is decisive for the meaning. It follows that neither knowledge nor science can be objective; they are, rather, the product of a number of subjective and inter-subjective conditions which must be specified.

The question of agreement between language and reality is of vital importance for our ability to find our bearings in the world, and it is thought-provoking that modern anthropological psychology emphasises the functional necessity of the human cognitive apparatus for the survival of the species. It is important for the human species to perceive language as a tool to be used to 'do something' to our environment in order to control it and make it serve our purposes.

This awareness of the intentionality of language and the consequent description of reality as an evaluation process is of immense importance to the study of law and legal decisions. As Gadamer points out, the umbilical cord uniting cognition to the practical concerns of human survival may work two ways. Just as knowledge and interpretation are dependent upon individual cases, the assessment of and decision on those individual cases depend on the interpretation of the wording of the legal rules and on the description of the facts in terms of those rules, i.e. on concretisation.

For a millennium, jurisprudence has striven to develop a theory of interpretation capable in practical terms of securing the individual person's legal rights and of predicting the outcome of a case with a degree of certainty. In this work, rhetoric and hermeneutics have proved excellent tools for lawyers. But when we lock and secure our front door, we risk burglars breaking in through an unsecured back door. This unsecured back door is the description or formulation of a factual occurrence in legal language, so that it may be inserted in the minor premise of the legal syllogism which constitutes the judicial decision. In fact, what this process requires us to do is to reclassify the raw facts of a specific case as generalisations framed in a legal language which we cannot use unless we relate it to the legal interpretation of the rules.

As Karl Engisch pointed out, this is a dialectical process whereby we systematically connect the wording and intention of the rule with the practical situation and the potential effects of the various interpretations of the practical situation. During this dialectic adaptation process, we want to consider repeatedly the pragmatic impact of a possible decision in light of the teleological content of the rule.

Although we should be careful of swallowing the practising lawyer's assertion that decisions are made intuitively and afterwards provided with a legitimate front to fit the rules, we must consider the possibility that like magicians, judges perform their judicial sleights of hand with reality, imposing a false sense of security on the parties by their use of the many precautions built into the interpretation of the rules of law.

ON CONCEPTS IN LAW

The analysis of legal concepts depends on which philosophy of science one adopts. A positivist theory will lead to a formula, an empty concept, which provides nothing more than terminological support, while a natural law theory will fill legal concepts with a substantive pre-legal content. A third route is the hermeneutic philosophy of language, which regards concepts as practical tools for a teleological and pluralistic theory of cognition and science. To illustrate the various approaches to legal concepts, I have chosen the concept of causation, which is central to all legal theory. But before proceeding, I shall provide a brief account of the concept of 'positivism', which is also used in various ways and for various purposes.

1. Positivism

The word and the concept of 'positivism' have been used and misused for many purposes. The literal meaning of the word is 'that which is given' (from *pono*), and when used in many ordinary and non-scientific and legal contexts, it is a positive word (positive in contrast to negative). In the scientific and university debate of the sixties, however, the word was used in the contrary sense, namely as the main enemy of 'progress', the social revolutions of that time having been legitimised through the adoption of a critical science in which positivism was perceived as a reactionary (and capitalist) means of oppression of the 'working classes' through the construction of a 'false consciousness', which took the existing (capitalist) society and its economic growth rationale for granted.

The logical-positivist theory of knowledge of the 1920s defined science partly as analytical statements and partly as assertions which are capable of verification: all other statements are 'metaphysical' or value judgments, a theory which assumes an objective scale and an objective language. The preceding idealist theory of cognition assumes an identity between language and the surrounding world, either because thought creates reality (subjective idealism) or because reality is logical (objective idealism).

Positivism was also posed in contrast to natural law, and presupposed, contrary to the latter, that law is the creation of man and not derived from metaphysical forces: God, reason, the ideal. While it was assumed in ancient times and in the Middle Ages that morality and law were derived from human nature (*zoon politikon*) through the use of reason, and while the rationalist theory of natural law of the Age of Enlightenment continued this tradition, the resulting theory of the constitutional state led to a legal positivism which could only legitimise the law via its constitutional theory of the separation of powers.

The concept of positivism thus touches on three different issues:

1. The theory of knowledge

2. The theory of law

3. Legal positivism

With respect to 1: Can science be expressed in objective language?
With respect to 2: Can lawyers speak authoritatively about moral requirements?
With respect to 3: Does the creation of all law require legislation?

a) *Language and reality*

Language is not a reflex reaction to, or a property of, things, from which it follows that it is meaningless to speak of a *necessary connection* (*rapports necessaires*) between object and action (*nature de chose, Natur der Sache*).

Every description is an interpretation because, like knowledge, language is *teleological* (determined by its purpose). Language is a cognitive tool on a par with other organs which contribute to the survival of the individual and the species, and it must be understood as a genetically-based means of communication belonging to the species, a tool which processes and communicates significant facts so that they can be transmitted to and processed by other individuals. Concepts and words therefore retain, necessarily, human values and objectives which cannot be removed. Language and cognition cannot be 'objective', but neither are they 'subjective', because a certain degree of *inter-subjectivity* is necessary for successful 'communication', i.e., for the transfer of a common conceptual content.

In other words, a *consistent positivist theory of knowledge* must be rejected for reasons of principle.

b) *The problem of natural law*

Lawyers use and describe the rules of law in terms of the criteria of validity applying to the particular legal system with which they are dealing, but lawyers have no political mandate to alter the rules of law. Both the courts and lawyers must therefore keep their own moral and *aesthetic judgments outside their application of the law*. In primitive societies it is not possible to distinguish between morality and law because, in such societies, custom identifies the applicable rules of law (*morality* from *mos – mores*: customs; *ethics* from *ethos*: customs). It is only with the emergence of modern society and the *political* function that the distinction between law and morals arises out of the emphasis placed by Renaissance man on the individual as the smallest unit of society, governed by society's supreme (law-making) will. The law is made by the society and enforced by its courts, while morality is a personal matter enforced by the court of conscience. *Natural law is the demand which morality makes on the court.*

In the moral philosophy of Antiquity and of the Middle Ages, both goodness and truth were considered to be properties inherent in any given action and capable of recognition through reason. This rationalist theory of natural law was continued in the Catholic moral philosophy of Europe in 1600-1700, until Hume's and Kant's critiques of reason led to the idealism and legal positivism of the Nineteenth Century.

c) *The constitutional state – the welfare state*

Legal positivism is a more recent legal theory which, in agreement with the principle of democratic government, equates law and state, and thereby identifies the concept of law with the actual laws adopted by parliaments (the will of the people). Legal positivism corresponds to the constitutional distribution of powers and has the *rule of law* as its basic value, in contrast to the modern welfare state's regulatory legislation, which has *instrumentalism* as its basic value and which uses various means, e.g. preambles, framework legislation, plans and guidelines to secure the greatest possible realisation of its political *objective*. It is self-evident that the law which existed before the constitution – to a broad extent the *law of custom* – must still apply unless revoked by parliament, and customary practice will still be an open source of law. Large parts of the legal system, for example the law of torts, have until recently had their most important source in customs and legal practice.

In recent times, *private creation of law* has gained increasing significance: company law and the law of associations is governed by private statutes and agreements, and labour law is a network of collective agreements, while the legal relationships in the world of business are widely governed with the aid of 'agreed documents', 'conventions', or standard terms which are 'adopted' either expressly or tacitly.

Legal positivism is not enough.

2. The concept of causation

'No more may be extracted from a concept than has already been put into it'. This was Knud Illum's principal argument (1945) against the old distinction between rights in property and chattels, on the one hand, and rights of obligation on the other. The first step had been, he said, to observe the legal status, and it was noted that rights in property and chattels could often be protected against creditors and other unsuspecting later acquirers of rights, while rights to money, i.e. financial claims, normally did not enjoy protection against third party. Rights to objects were consequently called proprietary interests, and financial claims were called rights of obligation, for which reason rights of ownership were systematically divided into the law of property and the law of obligations.

So far so good, but now a further step was taken which put the cart squarely before the horse: it now became permissible to draw conclusions about the protection of property from the type designation 'proprietary interests', while the designation 'rights of obligation' led to the conclusion that such rights offered no protection against third party without a 'binding individualisation'. The so-called *Begriffsjurisprudenz* (concept-based law) which dominated Continental jurisprudence in the early half of the Nineteenth Century took its point of departure in ordinary concepts and principles from which the solution to legal problems was then deduced relative to the intrinsic systematics which aimed at maintaining an exhaustive and contradiction-free context.

On the one hand this scientific method was a significant advance for jurisprudence. As for the empirical sciences, they could now, with the aid of definitions of concepts and their arrangements in a genus and species context, which justified binding logical conclusions, offer a reply to all questions within the system thus constructed. On the other hand, the method was separated from the reality which the law was to govern. The rule of law was quite obviously strengthened, but its applicability was highly limited.

This science model was borrowed from the Eighteenth Century rationalist theory of natural law, the first principles of which were based on the assumption of a common objective reason, which assumption was also transferred to morality and jurisprudence. As this assumption of a common objective reason and morality, which would provide an unambiguous answer when one thought enough about it, had to be abandoned following David Hume's and Immanuel Kant's critiques of reason, the legal system was derived instead from a set of general principles which were presumed to apply to all people, human society and the law. In private law, this was the principle of the individual person as the basic legal entity; in family law, the principle of association; and in national law, the principle of the state, which in general in the eyes of the liberal-conservative social philosophy of the time should play only a marginal role (the state as the night watchman). Freedom was society's highest goal, and humanity was the object for the state and not its means.

The principle of will therefore came to dominate the treatment of private law, which was the main area of concern for jurists at the time, and for good reasons, as the scope of the government and the state to undertake major domestic tasks was limited by economic factors. The original theory of knowledge assumed that the principles which govern the basic concepts must also govern the concepts and solutions derived from them. Aristotle's metaphysics was constructed on the distinction between essential and non-essential properties in accordance with his assertion that all entities have a *nature*, i.e., properties which define them and set them apart from all other things, and which they therefore strive to realise to the greatest extent possible. Since man's nature was *reason*, which separates him from other 'social animals', human actions can be considered as manifestations of this reason.

It was this rationalist outlook which, a couple of hundred years earlier, had started the speculative search of the Ionic natural philosophy for 'the infinite in the finite', and which, in the subsequent Hellenistic philosophy, led to formation of the 'systematic' textbook which gained very great significance for classical Roman law. The art of rhetoric taught the Romans to distinguish between *verba* and *voluntas*, and thus formed the basis of a hermeneutic theory of interpretation and the inspiration behind Gaius's textbook *Institutiones*.

The so-called glossators who founded Roman-derived jurisprudence at the northern Italian universities in the 1000s and 1100s saw their purpose as 'interpreting' *Corpus Iuris* as an authoritative text in agreement with the rhetoricians' ideal knowledge, i.e., on the basis of its external systematics, to create a whole by abolishing contradictions through *distinctiones* and filling lacunae through analogy. The canonical jurisprudence made use of the same methodology in its development of a dogmatic exegesis (laying out of authoritative texts), as contact with the Arab world had led to a renewed knowledge of Aristotle's metaphysics and logic. The goal and method (*met-odos* – 'the way by which') of Greek scholarship was reintroduced into Europe: *to* find the infinite in the finite, and *to* unite thought and reality, and hence to build certain and true knowledge. Later rationalism (Descartes) emphasised certainty, and empiricism (Galileo) truth – thus creating a dualism between which posterity attempted to mediate.

With the introduction of nominalism in the 1300s, the Aristotelian metaphysics of material concepts was abandoned, and science lost its teleological quality, according to which the 'nature' of things had been the object of research. No longer determined by its goal, science now (in accordance with the new world view) became occupied exclusively with the study of cause and effect. Jurisprudence was again joined to the social and political realities, and unlike previously, when the law was perceived as divine custom, it was now assumed that man could make law at will through temporal legislation and use it to attain political and social goals. Man had become a supreme being with the power to control the external (empirical) world through technology, and the internal (social) world through laws.

The problem of causation thus gained a prominent position in legal thinking with respect to both legislation and contractual and tort theory. While, in the old tribal society, the right of retribution had been the province of private law, it was now relegated through legislation to the status of an appendage to the royal powers, which included the maintenance of peace and justice, and was consequently financed principally through fines.

In the law of torts, which was gradually separated from criminal law, a wrong was assumed to trigger a claim for compensation for the loss. Under the influence of the church, however, this liability was gradually limited to the evil will, i.e., intention and negligence, while the question of compensation for accidental damage arose only in exceptional cases. During the rationalist natural law theory of the 1600s and 1700s, the doctrine of human supremacy gradually developed. In political terms, this is a demand for the people's competence to legislate, and, in terms of private law, it makes good will the basis for ordinary contract law, and evil will the cause of an ordinary *culpa* rule within tort law.

Both the contractual obligation and the obligation under tort law are limited to the consequences which can be foreseen by the players. This limitation is derived from the concept of will, which is assumed to underpin the private autonomy which governs all private law. Will must be limited to that which can be expected to follow; there is therefore no liability for 'unforeseeable' injurious consequences of acts which cause damage, and the obligations and content of the agreement are therefore limited to the 'assumptions' of the person who is liable. It follows that other consequences are not *caused* in a legal sense.

It is clear that the concept of system is no less important for the legal sciences than it is for science in general, since it is the presumption on which we base our use of scientific method, and hence the value placed in science on clarity and assurance. This is not, however, to say that the system concept is *decisive*, in the first place because major difficulties are associated with the conversion of concepts to real life application, and in the second place because it is necessary that there should always be a state of competition between rule and exception, between the rule of law and equity. Ever since Plato it has been a familiar dilemma for all rules which are to be applied to reality that the general limitations may lead to unfair results in specific situations. In contrast to the general concept, which is defined, the concept of the type is open and subject to value judgment.

The principal problem for epistemological theory is, however, the circumstance that language and reality belong to distinct logical categories, and that language and concepts do not exist in reality, but depict reality in the same manner as a photograph, which 'represents' a reality without being there. It follows that when a phenomenon belonging to the real world is 'called' by a name, an act of will is involved, a decision and not a logical conclusion; there is no necessary connection (*rapport necessaire*) – as Montesquieu and later thinkers in natural law believed – between concepts and reality (the nature of things, *nature de chose, Natur der Sache*).

Aristotle already knew the problem, which he treated in his second logic, where he drew attention to the fact that the underlying principles of the first logic cannot be derived from logic, but must be fixed by intuition (*nous*), and that it follows that reality must be framed in language and concepts before it can be treated scientifically. Later philosophy has attempted in many ways to overcome this dilemma, since a subjective (arbitrary) language frame will render science impossible. Language and the generating of concepts must thus be inter-subjective if they are to be used for a scientific purpose and for ordinary communication.

The idealism of the Nineteenth Century attempted to avoid the problem by assuming that we each create reality in our thoughts, which we then project out into space (subjective idealism), or by assuming that reality is already logically constituted (objective idealism – Hegel: reason is the real and the real is the rational). After many attacks on idealism around the turn of the Twentieth Century, a number of variants arose which have only one feature in common: they reject the existence of any objective correspondence between language and reality.

Intuitionism or phenomenology assumes that man possesses a special form of cognitive powers which enable him intuitively to comprehend both empirical phenomena and moral values, and to rank them in a systematic context. Existentialist philosophy rejects objectivity and makes subjectivity the truth, while pragmatism's criterion of truth is the consequences of the action. The English common law philosophy and the modern variant 'ordinary language philosophy' skip all formalities and make the daily language the genuine source of true knowledge.

It was in agreement with this analytical philosophy, dominant in the fifties, that Hart and Honoré in their book *Causation in the Law*, attempted to remove theory from the concept of cause. Analysing a number of judgments in which English courts had upheld or denied a legal liability, or 'causal connection', these authors believed that they had dealt with the concept of cause. However, daily language is not suited to solving complicated academic and scientific problems, and it also appears that the authors – unwittingly – committed the same conceptual error as conceptual jurisprudence, which confused concepts with reality. The action which the English courts took, and which all courts take, is to decide to assign liability for a particular consequence, which is then labelled as 'caused' by the action under judgment.

A more realistic approach is to perceive language 'pragmatically' in a slightly different sense than that of American instrumentalism, as recent linguistic philosophy and physiology have taught us to regard language as a tool on a par with our five senses and other biological and physiological reaction patterns which enter into the survival strategy of our genes. While signals are common to all species of animals (calls, warnings and reassurance), and, in social animals, also communication in connection with collective co-operative events such as hunting and care of the young, the human species has developed language as part of its survival strategy in connection with intelligence, upright posture, and a thumb which can grip and hold a tool. The difference between an aid, which many species of animals can use, and a tool, is the intelligent assumptions with respect to time and the individual which make it attractive to retain (and improve) an aid for later use, and thus to turn it into a tool. Language, which consists of concepts, i.e., generalised experiences, is therefore particularly suitable as a means of social communication and the storage of previous, shared, experiences which can be taught to subsequent generations and not merely imitated.

Language thus becomes an important tool in our treatment of reality and the social rules, for in naming things, we place values on phenomena and behaviour. All phenomena have a positive and a negative side. Aristotle himself described the different forms of control in this dualistic manner: one-man government: monarchy/tyranny; government by a small group:

aristocracy/oligarchy; government by the people: democracy/ ochlocracy. Individualism is not the same as egotism, and seen from different perspectives, a freedom fighter and a terrorist are different names for the same phenomenon.

It is strange that although this insight into the nature and function of language has been known since ancient times, it has only recently led to the understanding among scientists and especially legal scientists of the fundamental hermeneutic problem: to combine language and reality. The jurisprudence of the preceding 1000 years has attempted to limit arbitrariness in the application of the law by honing principles of language interpretation (word/meaning), interpretative tools (purpose, history, effect, analogy/contradiction, systematic arguments) and rules of conflict. On the whole, the history of rhetoric has been an attempt to make the 'true' meaning of the text real.

At the same time, the insight into the problematic relationship of reality to language has been allowed to rest in *claire-obscure* without anybody realising that to do so opened the application of the law to a significant level of arbitrariness through the framing in language of the 'raw' legal facts relative to the given legal rules. This is the very measure for the application of law, its touchstone as it were, but also its Achilles' heel. This is not to say, of course, that subjectivity and arbitrariness reign supreme, because in spite of everything, ordinary language has – and must have – a certain inter-subjectivity to be able to serve its purpose at all. To this it should be added that the teaching of the legal system and the corresponding professional ethos contribute to the profession's caring for the law to *the greatest possible extent*, but again only to the extent that is humanly possible.

In a debate on the use of judicial inquiries in the investigation of political matters, the president of the Danish supreme court said that while judges each have their own personal characteristics, which of course affect their way of handling and deciding a case, the characteristics of several judges balance one another collectively. In saying this he was not merely saying something about the fragility of judicial inquiries, but also something important about the voluntary nature of the legal decision and the possibilities of limiting its consequences.

To conclude with an anecdote, we can recall the tale of Pooh Bear and his visit to Rabbit, where he was stuck in the door – not because, as Rabbit said, Pooh had eaten too much, but because, as he himself asserted, the door was too narrow!

THE THEORY OF DOGMATICS

The theory of the relative or relationist concept of law was developed with constant reference to the methods of dogmatic legal science.

I became aware at an early stage that the writers representing a 'realist' legal science, supporting their rule of law by invoking 'public utility' and 'real considerations', were in fact still thinking in 'idealist' terms and only paying lip service to 'realism'. A closer analysis of their theories revealed that references to social considerations contained little more than references to general legal principles disguised as practical considerations. Nineteenth Century idealist legal science had sought the ethical 'legal basis' (contrary to the historical origins) of legal institutions and deduced the solution to concrete legal questions from this. As Kant in his critical theory had identified the 'concept of freedom' as the underlying value of private law, it followed that the principle that a promise is binding – because by making the promise, the promisor has declared his will to perform it – would apply not only to the whole of private law, but also to the individual private law disciplines and to the derivation of answers to concrete questions in private law.

Begriffsjurisprudenz, as this idealist legal science has been named, was developed in opposition to the Eighteenth Century's rationalist theory of natural law, but it took over all the important features of the natural law theory's methods, which had been largely a continuation of the scholastic methods of Medieval Romanist law. The hallmark of the scholastic method was its basis in authoritative texts (the Bible, *Corpus Iuris*, Aristotle and so on), the validity of which was unquestioned. Reason was the superior tool of cognition as the prevailing view since antiquity had been that there was no difference between theoretical and practical cognition. Given that man's nature or final cause was reason, human reason was able to decide objectively and immutably what was good and what was bad.

David Hume's and Immanuel Kant's critiques of knowledge had made it clear, however, that 'objective reason' is an illusion, and that scientific theoretical knowledge must be limited to the 'realm of necessity', i.e. the outside world, which must be understood to be ruled by causation, while ethical instrumental knowledge belonged to the 'realm of freedom', insofar as responsible human actions can only be derived from moral or legal norms. This was the fundamental separation of 'is' and 'ought'. Kant had based instrumental knowledge on freedom of action, the existence of which he was forced to hypothesise as the concept of responsibility would otherwise be meaningless. Consequently, the theory of law and ethics which came after Kant took the 'concept of freedom' as the basis for its construction of the private law system. Thus it came about that the methods of *Begriffsjurisprudenz* were practically identical to those of the natural law school. The aim of both schools was to seek the rational 'legal basis' of every legal institution and then derive the concrete legal questions as effects of the 'legal basis' or 'legal doctrine'.

Around the mid-Nineteenth Century, a fundamental change took place in the methods applied in Danish (Scandinavian) legal science. Out of private law in personal, family and inheritance law, which was still founded on the principle of legal capacity and the principle that a promise is binding because the promisor, by giving the promise, has declared his will to perform it, the law of property was isolated for special treatment with reference to the 'social principle' and the interest of 'circulation'. Following this, the 'principle of objective interpretation' was developed as the decisive principle for ordering the rules of the law of property. In contrast to the principle of binding promises, which asks about the promisor's intentions or will, and thus about his interest in being bound, the principle of objective interpretation looks instead to joint contracting parties' and third parties' expectations and interests as its basis for solving concrete questions of law.

Although the purpose had been to return to Ørsted's 'realist' legal theory with its focus on the 'nature of the case' as the most important tool in law, the methodological principle remained the same. All that had happened was that the base of the argument had shifted from the agent to the expectations of the surrounding world. The method had not changed. The task continued to be that of deriving individual solutions from the correct principle. It was not until Viggo Bentzon's realist legal philosophy around the turn of the century (1907) that Ørsted's ideas became reality with Bentzon's advocacy of an 'empirical' legal sources theory. Bentzon later revised his theory, attempting to unite the interests of opinion and rule by demanding that the judicial decision be made on the basis of concrete justice, but in a manner reconcilable with the need for the decision to serve as a model for future decisions. Alf Ross and Knud Illum were later to develop this theory further.

Scandinavian realism soon met opposition with Alf Ross's vehement attack in the forties on Vilhelm Lundstedt's (1930) variant in particular. In Ross's opinion, Lundstedt's theory was exploiting 'public utility' in the same way that Lundstedt in his younger days, before becoming aware of Axel Hägerström's critique of idealism, had exploited *Begriffsjurisprudenz* principles. 'Justice' had merely been renamed 'public utility'. The result remained the same, namely that the dogmatist unconsciously came to his decisions on the basis of his own evaluations and then legitimised them by referring to a general 'principle' or 'consideration' which was so abstract that it could be used to legitimise any decision whatsoever. Knud Illum directed the same criticism against Frederik Vinding Kruse's formal reference to 'the demands of practical life' (1943) as another instance of disguised idealism scantily covered in the cloak of realism.

This double inspiration was to become decisive for the development of my own views in my work on the law of torts and the law of contracts. In my student days, I had already, in an examination paper, taken a critical attitude towards the 'principle of implied conditions' in the law of contracts as formulated by Henry Ussing (1918), and it was hardly by chance that my first major scientific attempt was a criticism of the principle of adequacy in the law of torts, a principle not unlike 'foreseeability' but impinging on cause rather than liability. The main points of my criticism of these and other general principles, e.g. the principles of 'wrongfulness' (*Rechtswidrigkeit*) and of 'negligence', were firstly that Henry Ussing's 'law of obligation', formally based on instrumental concerns, was still anchored in the Nineteenth Century idealist philosophy of law, and secondly that the above principles were not merely a dogmatic generalisation of individual rules and individual decisions but, on the contrary, legal doctrines of which the individual rules and concrete decisions were regarded as 'manifestations'. This was most obvious when Ussing wanted to regard large parts of contract law, both the Contract Act's invalidity rules and the rules governing breach of contract in the Sale of Goods Act, as manifestations of the principle of implied conditions, and when he regarded the material principle of 'wrongfulness' as normative for several of the constituent questions in the law of torts.

The crucial point of my criticism of Ussing's use of these general principles was that it led to rationalist methods and not to the realist methods which his reference to 'instrumental considerations' formally assumed. This problem was particularly acute in cases where Ussing referred to one 'instrumental consideration' as '*the* instrumental consideration' for a particular branch of law. This formulation has the effect of changing the method so it becomes 'monistic' rather than 'pluralist', where the latter term implies acknowledgement of the fact that conflicting 'instrumental considerations' can lead to different results in different 'relationships'. The 'relationist' theory of law which I later arrived at should thus be regarded as a further development of my early criticism of dogmatics.

With inspiration from the methods of German *Begriffsjurisprudenz*, attempts were made on the basis of the principles of wrongfulness and adequacy to construct a theory on the limitations applying to individual freedom of action and, conversely, on the scope of liability for violation of freedom of action. The theory of implied conditions was similarly inspired by Windscheid and concerned the scope of obligations in the law of contracts. Based on the general assumption that obligation is derived from the agent's will, the method required the lawyer to find 'justification' in the same principle, also with regard to the individual rules of contract law and torts. It followed from this that the agent's 'implied conditions' and the 'foreseeability' of later developments came to the fore in the development of special rules on the consequences of contract and tortious acts.

As far as the principles of wrongfulness and adequacy are concerned, such a development is understandable, as these theories are primarily the work of criminal lawyers who have the entire criminal law and the law of torts as their area. As far as the law of implied conditions is concerned it was less understandable, as it was clear that the Scandinavian law of contracts had distanced itself from the German theory of volition and had developed a theory of objective interpretation, the main emphasis of which was placed on the expectations of third parties, which is why the agent's implied conditions were not an obvious criterion for the extent of his obligations.

But a closer analysis and description of the law of damages in tort revealed that in contrast to criminal law, the interest of the injured party constituted an important consideration, as the very object of the law of torts was to decide whether the tortfeasor or the injured party should bear the risk of loss. In other words, it is not only the interests of the tortfeasor but also those of the injured party which must be taken into account. 'Deterrence', as the legal interest is called which has come to be regarded as the basis of criminal law, must here compete with the interest of 'reparation'. Deterrence can be divided into general deterrence and special deterrence, and is another way of expressing the fact that tort law contains an 'obligation' to limit damage to other people's persons or things. General deterrence, which stands for the deterring and normative effect, expresses this compliance with the rule concept, while special deterrence, the motivation underlying concrete behaviour, has less importance, particularly after third-party insurance has become common.

The justification for right of action has undergone several changes during the course of legal history, moving from an objective and collective basis to a subjective and individualistic view. Having been divided in more recent times into a public penal law and a private law of torts, the specialised law of torts has changed similarly. While, during the Middle Ages, the general rule was that the tortfeasor and his family bore the risk of loss on an objective basis, the general distribution of risk in the Nineteenth Century tended merely to prescribe responsibility for negligence (*culpa*). Later, with the spread of technology and insurance, the risk came increasingly to be distributed on an objective basis.

In the Nineteenth Century's liberal society, the general rule was that a person was only liable for damages if he or she had acted 'wrongfully' (contrary to the rights of others) and dangerously in a manner such that the person could have foreseen, and thus avoided the injurious consequences of the action. As mentioned above, the rule was divided into a principle of wrongfulness and a principle of culpability. The principle of wrongfulness was based on interests of law and order, and prescribed that an action could incur liability in the interest of the protectors of the assets only if it had been foreseeable that it would overstep the limits of freedom of action. On the other hand, negligence was a rule of liability for foreseeable and preventable injuries, while finally, the principle of adequacy limited liability to injuries resulting from foreseeable consequences.

I criticised both this triple 'foreseeability assessment', and foreseeability itself as a criterion for deciding on wrongfulness and negligence and as a criterion for the limits of liability, arguing instead that a genuine 'realist' method must begin by setting up different relationships. The law of torts cannot be formulated as a choice between negligence and risk, because the rule of negligence itself is an expression of a distribution of risk. Any assessment of the constituent areas of the law of torts similarly depends upon a legal and political evaluation of the various sub-questions.

It had already been recognised that the rule of damages only applied to injuries to persons or things, whereas 'general property damage' must be compensated according to the special conditions applying within the various areas, often as premeditated or criminal behaviour. Similarly, it was only 'financial' injury which could be compensated under the general rule of damages, while special rules applied to 'non-financial' injuries. It was generally recognised that the questions

1.   Which interests are protected by the rule of damages?

2.   Which persons can claim damages?

3.   Which advantages must be offset in the loss?

must be decided by assessing the practical considerations in the individual relationships. I believe that the same must also apply to the remaining areas, so that the question of adequacy would be divided into different relationships:

1.   On the one hand, damage to things; and, on the other, injuries to persons.

2.   The initial injury, on the one hand, and consequential injuries on the other.

3.   The fairness of costs paid and assessment of loss.

4.   The influence of the time factor and possibility of evidence.

5.   The injured party's intervention and the fairness of this.

6.   Competing accidental and actionable causal factors etc.

It was difficult on the whole to reconcile the decisions in these various relationships and constellations with any general formulation of 'adequacy', which must therefore be regarded as a label covering the 'fair' order of priority for the interests of the parties and the society involved in the conflict. Just as adequacy was divided into its various relationships and ended as a synthesis of these relationships, wrongfulness was reduced to a formal label for the conditions which exclude a responsibility for damages:

1. Self-defence, *jus necessitatis*.

2. Consent (as far as this is possible).

3. Omission (only in cases where there is an 'obligation to act').

The foreseeability and deterrence labels within the principle of *culpa*, and the balancing of interests under the umbrella of wrongfulness, could be paraphrased as a general search for the source of law: the decisive test of liability must be whether a general norm of action, official or customary, had been violated.

To sum up, the main point in my criticism of the theory of the law of torts was that despite its realistic surface quality, it was still bound to the idealist method of the Nineteenth Century, with the main emphasis being on the parties' subjective expectations and not on objective legal considerations. As mentioned, similar criticisms applied to the law of contracts, where Henry Ussing had seen the theory of implied conditions as a general legal principle from which the rules of contracts and of obligations were both derived. This was even more odd in that it was precisely one of the great advances of the Scandinavian theory of private law that the law of property had been separated from the law of person, and thereby removed from the principle of binding promises and subjected to the principle of objective interpretation, and thus to considerations of the interests of circulation and trade.

The principle of implied conditions to which Ussing subscribed was, indeed, also an 'objective' theory, in contrast to Julius Lassen's 'subjective' principle (1892). It was not an individual test of the parties' 'hypothetical will' which was to decide the validity of the contract and the extent of obligation (tacit conditions as limitations of will) but, on the contrary, the 'condition usually implied'. The parties must usually assume the risk for individual assumptions themselves, unless the obligation had been made conditional upon these assumptions, or unless it was evident to the promisee that an individual assumption was determinative for his transaction. Even in cases where such an individual assumption, evident to the other contracting party, was decisive for the transaction, it could only be considered a significant condition if special grounds existed for imposing the 'risk' of its failure upon the opposite party. It was clear to Ussing that a contrary solution would jeopardise trade because no transaction incurring loss would otherwise be binding, as the profit motive must evidently be determinative for every businessman.

Ussing considered, moreover, the type condition and the 'relevant' conditions as identical with the so-called 'supplementary legal rules'. These rules must supplement all agreements of a certain type by specifying what to do in the event of an unexpected and abnormal development in the contractual relationship of a kind which has not as a rule been taken into consideration. As mentioned, Ussing saw the entire rule set on breach of contract as 'derived' from the principle of 'implied conditions', which is the reason why the rules of specific performance, damages in contract, and the rules of rescission and proportional reduction for defects must be understood and interpreted in accordance with the structure and conditions of the principle of implied conditions, notwithstanding the fact that these problems were already regulated by specific legislation, particularly in the Sale of Goods Act and the Contracts Act.

In my view it was wrong to attempt to interpret positive legal provisions in light of a theory which not only predates the two acts, but which had also been either rejected or ignored in the acts' motives. It should have been assumed instead that the positive legislation had itself decided the 'question of relevance' and performed that balancing of interests which the principle of implied conditions intends. Added to this was the fact that Ussing's 'principle of implied conditions' was inspired by Ernst Møller (1894), who had formulated his theory before the Scandinavian Sale of Goods Act and Contracts Act were enacted.

In agreement with Knud Illum's criticism in particular, I was forced to regard the theory of implied conditions as a circumlocution, an unfounded attempt at connecting the legal effects of the parties' agreements to their own expectations, and not to objective legal considerations. It would be preferable, in my view, to begin by setting out the general principles of legal interpretation and then, in cases of conflict or interpretative doubts, give priority firstly to specific legislation: the rules of contracts and tort, including the Sale of Goods Act, above the general law of contracts. This would, for example, apply to the interpretation of fraud, which can involve invalidity, but can also give grounds for annulment of the contract, and the difference in compensation attendant upon the interpretation (reliance damages/expectation damages). Secondly, the individual contract must be subjected to direct interpretation and a decision reached as to which interpretation would be 'better justified', and the requisite legal effects derived by recourse to supplementary general law rules.

There is no need for a principle of implied conditions side by side with general legal interpretation and the interpretation of contracts. It militates to some extent against general legal interpretation. Moreover, the attempt to derive legal effects from the parties' expectations rather than from objective legal considerations belongs to an antiquated philosophy and method. The terminology is, however, still in use in legal practice, although it is unclear whether the term 'implied condition' is used in a psychological sense synonymous with expectations, or in a technical sense, as the principle implies. The principle has also been rejected in more recent Norwegian and Swedish theories, although some have invoked it as 'authority' for rules of invalidity which Danish legal practice – and even Henry Ussing – have arrived at by analogy with the Contracts Act, without recourse to the principle of implied conditions. Among these invalidity rules is the rule that a party is liable for any incorrect information which he advances in good faith, thereby causing the other party to act. After the amendment of the Contracts Act to include the clause which allows 'unreasonable' contract terms to be set aside, there is no need whatsoever for the principle of implied conditions, particularly if it is acknowledged that the rule not only allows the setting aside of terms, but also a general regulation of contracts.

In terms of method, such an attitude to the principle of implied conditions corresponds to the relationist method which I have pleaded for above. The fact that as an institution, the law of contracts is based on the autonomy of the parties, and assumes an individualist and liberalist view of man and society, cannot justify the assumption that its legal effects can in general be derived from the intentions or expectations of the parties. The legal effects must, where there is no opinion, be derived from objective legal considerations which vary from relationship to relationship.

Looked at from a functional point of view, the contract is a subjective means used in developed societies for arranging the necessary distribution of goods, which in other more primitive societies is arranged through objective status relationships which secure the individual his or her share of the collective production. Reciprocity is the material basis for the law of contracts, and in our modern society, objective facts and standard agreements have superseded the individual agreement as the 'social type' for the framing of the rules of contract law. Objective facts and the assessment of a reasonable level of reciprocity have come more to the fore, particularly in the so-called consumer relationships where mandatory rules aim to secure a reasonable level of reciprocity in the interests of the consumer.

Conversely, in commercial relationships, a new private legal basis has been provided through 'agreed documents', i.e. standard documents, and 'conventions' established by negotiations among national and international organisations. In interpreting such a 'private creation of law', it is, on the other hand, natural to use general objective methods of legal interpretation instead of a subjective interpretation of contract.

DOGMATICS AND EMPIRICISM

Sliced bread is invented once every generation, a fact for which we can thank the innocence of ignorance.

In 1968 the Swedish professor Per Olof Bolding invented something which he called the 'social sciences' theory', his theory being that the study of law and the application of law is not a consequence of authoritarian rules, but the result of a political debate. This theory was of course first and foremost an offshoot from Swedish realism, but it also carried clear reminiscences of the 'sociology of law' called *Freirecht* from the turn of the century, and of the popular post-war 'existentialist' schools of legal thought. Rules are not general standards, but merely possible solutions from which the individual decision-maker makes his choice in every particular instance.

Alf Ross's theory also showed this decisionist element, refusing to recognise the validity of general standards. Ross refused to speak of 'valid' law, preferring the term 'current' law, and his book *On Law and Justice* was an analysis of concepts and methods of legal science and not of law. The verification and prediction apparatus was an important outcome of his logical positivist theory, and this meant that 'semantic reference' became a key concept for, according to Ross, scientific statements were meaningful only if they were able to point to 'something' which corresponded to the 'language content' of the statement. All the rest was metaphysics or nonsense.

Quite apart from the fact that this theory presupposed an objective language content which does not exist, according to a hermeneutic theory of language it was, as Vilhelm Aubert pointed out, a sociology of law rather than a theory of law (1943).

The same applied to the 'democratic' legal theories which arose in the sixties in opposition to Hans Kelsen's and Max

Weber's centralist theory of the state. The Polish legal sociologist Adam Podgorecki (1974) became known for his 'polycentricity' theory, i.e. a theory of legislative pluralism which claims that laws are not only made by dedicated legislative bodies, but also in private organisations based on agreements and, not least, custom.

On the basis of various legal and political ideologies, Jürgen Habermas's 'discursive theory', Niklas Luhmann's *autopoietic* theory and Gunther Teubner's 'reflexive theory of law' have added new perspectives to the various functions of the law identified by the sociology of law. J. Dalberg-Larsen has found a connection between authoritarian political systems and theories of legal commands, while there appears to be a connection between 'sociological' theories and liberal political issues (*Retsvidenskaben som Samfundsvidenskab*, 1977).

The study of sources of law has always been 'polycentric', as the law has had multiple 'sources' throughout modern times. This is probably the reason why it tends to be constitutional lawyers who, like Hans Kelsen, assume a comprehensive system of sources starting with a 'basic norm', or others who, starting with the same basic assumption, claim that the formulation of a polycentric theory of law or theory of sources of law is something new and very special.

The various sociological function theories have not, however, been able to remove the normative validity element from legal dogmatics entirely. It is not unimportant whether the law is perceived as a duty or as a feeling of duty. The law has both a normative and a practical side, one of which cannot replace the other. While belonging to distinct logical categories like language and reality, they are two sides of the same coin.

This is why legal scientists cannot be satisfied with a sociological theory alone, but must include both the normative and the descriptive aspects in their accounts. This is why the science of law must be pluralistic, because the law has different 'producers of norms' and different 'receivers of norms' in both historical and practical terms.

In primitive societies, the law is 'reflexive', custom being the only, or at any rate the all-dominant, source of law. The idea that man has the power to make laws appears at a relatively late stage in social development, evolving from the dual competence of king and church in the Middle Ages to an ideological state monopoly in the Nineteenth Century. Hans Kelsen's and Karl Schmitt's (1934) theories of law had a decisive influence on contemporary fascist and communist theories of law in the 30s, but were also fundamental to the development of the western world's welfare state theory (Lundstedt, Ross) in opposition to Weber's constitutional state theory.

Steward McCauly (1986) drew attention to the breakdown of the official legal system as early as 1963, when demonstrating that the business sector was making increasing use of informal conflict resolutions while rejecting the choice of public court actions. The business sector can simply afford neither the time nor the money. Even less can they afford to risk the outcome and the potential loss of goodwill in an economic system which turns everybody into colleagues or competitors.

The 'expediency' of the welfare state is gradually again finding itself in competition with the constitutional government's interest in protecting the due process of law, as the poor become financial and legal partners and opponents, thus depriving lawmakers of part of their hold on their minds. 'Deregulation' or 'privatisation' are becoming politically distinct keywords which stress the element of individualism, and hence human rights, and the attending concern for the due process of law.

Legal theory is not only 'polycentric', i.e. there are several different senders of norms, it is first and foremost 'pluralist', insofar as the law has a number of functions which must be able to be contained in one general concept of law. The law is 'polycentric' insofar as law is generated both publicly and privately, and it is both 'directive' and 'reflexive' insofar as the law is an expression of both human consciousness and inarticulate customs. I have often used the story of the six blind men who, when asked to define an elephant, caught hold of different parts of its body, thus deciding in turn that it was a column, a sword, a blanket, a whip, a wall and a thunderclap.

CONTRACT AND DELICT

People in primitive societies think in concrete, casuistic, collective and objective terms.

Primitive societies therefore have no rules on binding contracts or individual responsibility. Law enforcement is limited to physical revenge on the outside group which wronged a member of one's own group. It is a common trait found in all known written laws from ancient times – and a sign of the emergence of a more civilised society – that revenge is replaced by penalties and that 'the law' becomes essentially a penalty catalogue listing various offences against the integrity of person and property. The general assumption is that these penalty rates were the result of a series of negotiation and arbitration decisions arising from the types of conflict brought before a forum of 'thingmen' in the broadest possible sense.

It is therefore also commonly held that like morality, 'law' developed out of custom (*mos – ethos*) and that the conflict and the action predate the rule, and hence the action type system. This is how Roman law was constituted throughout its history (the action system), as was the British common law in medieval England (the writ system). Contract law thus consists of a system of rights of action (*locus standi*) which make certain practical types of transactions enforceable by stipulating the penalty for breach of an 'obligation'. The underlying principle of contract law is thus the right of action, as is most clearly seen in the British development of *assumpsit*, the tool used in the Medieval period for deriving rights from obligations within a contractual relationship. The reason why the Roman legal process, like the British, always ends in a *condemnatio* involving money is to be found in this underlying principle of enforceable law.

Another common feature of Roman and British contractual law is the principle of consideration or *causa* in Latin. 'An Englishman is not bound because he has made a promise, but because he has made a bargain'. One thing in return for another, reciprocity, quid pro quo is the rational basis on which substantive contract law builds. One-sided promises are only binding if they have been entered into with the aid of special forms or formulae (*stipulatio*, seal [deed]).

It was only with the emergence of rationalist natural law theory in the Seventeenth and Eighteenth Centuries that the individual and individualism achieved full ascendancy. With this theory, the individual will or intentions become the source of law, good intentions constituting the contractual rights and obligations, and bad intentions the justification for right of action on the grounds of the guilt of the offender. In the second half of the Eighteenth Century, the general law of contract was based on consensus (the meeting of minds, cf. DL 5-1-1) and the general law of tort sprang from the culpa principle; '*Keine Übel ohne Schuld*', as Ihering wrote in 1871.

In other words, the law of contract and the law of tort have evolved via the same conceptual development process from a collective and objective status organisation in which honour and revenge were the cogs in the wheel of legal action and in which specified rights to take legal action constituted the primary element of an individualistic consensus ideology based on personal will or intentions, good intentions in contract theory and evil intentions in the law of delict. The social model corresponding to this theory was the social equilibrium and liberalism of the Age of Enlightenment, as expressed in Kant's theory of cognition and ethics in the late Eighteenth Century.

In the course of the Nineteenth Century it became clear, however, that the law is not merely a question of the power of the will arising from a reasoned debate among enlightened persons. With the emergence of the technological revolution and the class society, the liberal social equilibrium was gradually displaced by the recognition that the law is the outcome of warring interests within society, and that the general good and not the general will is the goal society is striving towards. The year before Ihering wrote his famous pamphlet *Das Schuld-moment im Römischen Recht* under the slogan *'Keine Übel ohne Schuld'* (1871), the Prussian Railroads had introduced strict liability for the new railroads.

Spurred by this development, Henry Ussing argued a case for general strict liability for 'dangerous operations' in 1914, while maintaining his support for the previous generation's liberal legal conflict theory and its weighing of the elements of risk of injury or damage against utility. As early as the 1890s, the Danish courts had imposed strict liability on employers, supplemented by a statutory accident insurance for employees, and around the turn of the century and in the early decades of the Twentieth Century, strict liability or a presumption of negligence was imposed by law on railroads, motor vehicles, air traffic and power plants, but no general rule concerning 'dangerous operations' found support in the courts, which went no further than to require a more rigorous duty of care, especially with regard to professional activities.

A state approaching strict liability in the proper sense òf the word only applies in cases involving failure of materials, public traffic systems or various public utilities systems. The introduction of a professional responsibility concept in the courts led to a corresponding tightening of the exemption rules contained in the Danish Insurance Contracts Act, *FAL* Section 25, and the Act on liability in tort, *EAL* Section 19 and others, which effectively transferred the exposure hazard from the injured party's property insurance to the professional liability insurance.

The contract was one of the elements which imposed obligations on individual persons of a kind which they would not generally have, obligations to protect the interests of others and which therefore involve the person thus bound in contractual liability for the breach of his or her obligations, a liability which was often imposed beyond the level of *culpa* in business or professional relationships. Although product liability is not covered by the provisions on liability for defects in the Sale of Goods Act, a case law developed during the early half-century, establishing liability for the 'hazardous properties' of a service provided. The liability also applied to third party.

Product liability was strengthened so much by the courts as to constitute a *de facto* state of presumed negligence with regard to defects, such that the introduction of the Product Liability Act of 1989 (*PAL*) meant only a marginal tightening of the *status quo* despite the Act's introduction of strict liability for defects. This particular step to increase product liability for defects in goods or services was to have considerable influence on the development of professional liability, which imposes stricter liability on the members of various liberal professions for defects in the performance of their professional duties. Medical practitioners and hospital treatment in particular are bound by such professional liability based on stringent quality criteria. The most recent development has been directed at financial advisory services, where a long series of obligations and extensive liability for defects have been imposed on real estate agents, including liability for any error on their part with regard to the presentation of a property's budget and financing. On this basis, disappointed clients have also attempted to make banks and other financial advisers responsible for erroneous calculations, even if the error did not involve 'injury', as the client obtained the best possible deal. Instead, the Credit Institutions Complaints Board has paid out compensation for 'disappointed hopes', a construction which has been rejected by the courts. The question has been passed to a legislative committee which has failed to agree on a proposal on the issue, among other reasons because it is a hybrid construction which is difficult to harmonise with a civil law system.

Instead, it is my recommendation that the bank be considered as an ordinary tenderer who is bound by his tender in his relationship with his client – despite the fact that the tender promises more than is usual – as long as the client is acting in good faith, and this would generally apply to a private person in dealings with a professional financier (Section 32 of the Act on Contracts). This line of argument would similarly apply to those who supply share ownership projects on a professional basis or offer other options on financial undertakings to a broad market or sections thereof.

We see here how contract law and the law of tort are con-

verging again, having for centuries moved further and further
apart from their common starting point and standing utterly
apart during the Age of Enlightenment, joined only by the same
individualistic doctrine of the will. We must not forget, however, that contract law and the law of delict both have roots in
the general principle of justice deriving from the Classical
doctrine of relative or commutative justice, which sees equilibrium as the general legal principle under which performance
must be matched by consideration in contract law while the
right of action must be matched by the wrong under the law of
tort.

This doctrine of substantive justice is generally the practical
measure for both contract law and the law of delict. The
practical question is therefore how we divide the risk of loss
both inside and outside contractual relationships. Should it be
culpa or a more strict liability, with the contractual elements
being one of the factors affecting the assessment of liability,
insofar as the contract imposes obligations on the parties which
they did not already have, and departs from the doctrine of the
will as happens currently in situations where considerations
regarding third parties require protection of the promisee's
'good faith' or 'justified expectations'?

In cases involving 'consumer contracts' in the broadest sense
of the term, there are particularly good reasons to bend far
towards protecting expectations of a kind which the professional
adviser is the obvious person to understand and advise about,
and the risk can be limited through both pricing and insurance.
In the world in which we live, contracts are not normally the
result of a deliberately calculated advantage and risk negotiated
between equal parties, but the result of a person entering
general contractual terms or, on a more rudimentary level, a
non-verbal exchange of goods and services in supermarkets and
other typical social relations of a 'quasi-contractual' nature such
as entering a means of public transport, a car park etc. In all
these cases it would often seem an arbitrary choice whether we
label an action for damages as a claim regarding a contractual
right to a service or as a claim for damages in tort or contract
law.

PROPORTIONALITY

When all is said and done, the proportionality principle is merely a practical application of Kant's liberal ethics and social philosophy. Kant based his philosophy on a belief in individualism and the existence of free will, both as postulate and as a logical condition for the existence of law and morals (practical reason). If human beings have no free will, it becomes an absurdity to speak of responsibility, just as the outside world cannot exist without causality (pure reason).

The logical assumption with regard to ethics and law is therefore that individual freedom must be limited by other people's equal right to freedom according to general rules. While earlier natural law theory had placed the restriction on individual freedom and rights in metaphysical powers such as Rousseau's 'true common will' or the 'social contract', Kant and Hume rejected these constructs by pointing out that it is not society that thinks and feels, but individual human beings, and that it is therefore necessary that an external positive authority assume the role of lawmaker. This is the point where the state enters history as the positive authority entrusted with the powers of lawmaking and identified by the system of rules by which it is constituted. As Hans Kelsen was later to put it, the state and the law are two sides of the same coin.

As was the case with the 1960s principle of equality, the main importance of the 1990s proportionality principle was as a general doctrine of law in administrative and national law. A legal doctrine is a general concept of law which underpins the legal system without being formally a part of it and which defines the framework for legal argumentation.

It is now recognised that the question regarding the status of sources of law as binding materials, in contrast to legal argu-

mentation which constitutes *permissible* arguments in the legal
decision making process, is more complicated than generally
assumed. It is not possible to separate sources of law from their
'interpretation', as all language events must be interpreted in
order to fulfil their function as meaningful communication.
Neither is it possible to compare the interpretations of written
messages, as different methods must be used for each message
depending on its purpose. The purpose of a work of art or of a
set of minutes is different from the purpose of a rule of law.
While the recipient's experience is the most important purpose
of a literary text, the sender's purpose is the basis of the interpretation of a social norm, including rules of law, insofar as its
intended meaning is to control the recipient's behaviour. The
social purpose must never, therefore, be forgotten in the interpretation of a legal rule, and the interpretation must be based on
the constitutional ideology underpinning the state's legal system. It is equally necessary to keep in mind the consequences
which the state ideology will have for the interpretation of the
various areas of law, personal autonomy in private law, the
legality principle in administrative law and the protection of
individual rights in criminal and procedural law.

To understand the status enjoyed by the proportionality
principle, we must, however, trace its roots even further back in
the history of civilisation and even higher up in the hierarchy of
meta-legal principles. In historical terms, we must return to
Aristotle's theory of law, according to which commutative or
corrective justice along with *isonomy* (equality before the law)
are the oldest legal doctrines governing all human societies.
These doctrines require proportionality between performance
and consideration and between crime and retribution. In primitive societies, where law enforcement is dominated by a revenge
which is basically unlimited in scope, this revenge is gradually
reduced to *talion* (an eye for an eye), and ultimately replaced by
penalties according to a customary penalty catalogue. National
law philosophy is similarly based on the idea of a 'social contract' which dominate ethics and natural law theory from the
Middle Ages until the rise of modern democracies. In more
developed societies, commutative justice is supplemented by

distributive justice, which is based on society's assessment of the value of an act. To this should finally be added equity (*aequitas*), which must be considered every time a general rule is applied to a specific instance by ranking the various interests: teleology (purpose), pragmatism (particular interests) and *isonomy* (due process of law). A court decision is not a logical process but an alogical one, as norm and reality belong to distinct categories of logic which require language qualification of the actual facts before they can enter into a legal event and into a language syllogism.

Isonomy expresses the primary demand of justice insofar as it allows people to plan and build their lives according to 'justified expectations', expectations which arise from the doctrine that like cases must be treated alike according to rule. This doctrine sets western legal theory apart from the so-called *cadi* justice of totalitarian societies, which means that the head of state (the leader), religion (the Koran), or an ideology (Communism) is responsible for law and order.

The highest principle in Greek thinking was the concept of *harmonia*, 'to each his own', and the belief that exaggeration incurs the wrath of the gods. Adopting the Greek stoical philosophy with its underpinning doctrine of equality, Roman law rested on a three-point requirement as summarised by Celsus: live honestly, harm nobody, and give each what rightfully belongs to him. Classical Roman law also tore itself loose from the ancient system of magic-religious formulae and rituals and developed a fundamental distinction between *verba* and *voluntas* (word and meaning) in both contract and procedural law, although it never reached the point of complete recognition of contractual freedom or a general *culpa* rule in tort.

Medieval civil law ethics was based on the concepts of reciprocity and *justum pretium*, i.e. there must be a balance between goods provided and payment in return, in the sense that any reduction in the provision of goods carries a proportionate reduction in payment. This principle underwent further development and elaboration in the later rationalist natural law theory of the Seventeenth Century. In contract law, invalidation rules had been developed in classical Antiquity for setting aside valid agreements if they had been entered into on the basis of coercion, fraud or error. *Minor* irregularities which had no impact on the promise could not, however, invalidate a contract. The same applied to circumstances which were not 'unlawful' or 'dishonest' (in contrast to coercion or fraud). To find the fine line between justified trading practices and unjustified mis-representation, it is necessary to weigh different interests one against the other in accordance with the general ethics of the industry involved. In criminal law and the law of tort, the definition of self defence and necessity similarly depends on the weighing of opposing interests (the steps taken must be reasonable under the circumstances), as is also the case with police powers.

One might say that the proportionality principle has always been an integral part of western legal philosophy and that it does not constitute a separate constitutional doctrine. It is, however, only recently that constitutional lawyers have realised that the individual human rights are part of the history of western civilisation and must therefore be seen not as absolutes but as relative rights, insofar as they can, in certain areas, come into conflict with one another, and must therefore be weighed and ranked with reference to the same essential interests which apply to all our other legal doctrines and their applications. The Court of Human Rights' decision in the so-called Jersild case illustrates this realisation in its rejection of the claim of 'racism' with reference to the 'freedom of speech' which the Court deemed to be more important in the particular case.

The proportionality principle is thus an expression of an ancient and fundamental western legal doctrine which warns us of the belief that a simple logical language interpretation of an abstract rule will give us an unambiguous answer to a question of law. To the lawyer, the internalised 'proportionality principle' is part of our historical heritage, an anchorage protecting the application of law against fundamentalism, pedantry and sophistry, forces capable of wrecking any 'reasonable' application of law. In the words of Viggo Bentzon: 'The rule has its place, but judgment must never give way' (*Skøn og Regel* 1914).

LAW AS A STANDARDISING SYSTEM

Of all standardising systems, law is the oldest one. No society is possible without a system of rules to ensure that its members' expectations of behaviour will be fulfilled, as every act of co-operation requires predictability of its members' obligations, i.e. promises to do or to abstain from doing something.

In primitive societies, expectations of behaviour are regulated by customs, the foundation of which is status relations (in the clan or the family) generally decided with reference to religion or ritual. Until the second half of the Thirteenth Century, the conception of law in Western Europe was that the rules of law originated from a divine custom which could be changed only by the Church, as the Church alone was able to interpret divine law when it was not clearly manifest in the form of a custom. Collections of laws of the Twelfth and Thirteenth Centuries were records of customary law after the same pattern as the contemporary records of Canon Law.

With the rise of individualism in the Renaissance, a secular and instrumental belief evolved in the sovereignty of man to alter his physical world by means of science and technology and his social world through legislation, as a result of which a new instrumental legislative power came into being during the Fourteenth Century. This new technological, scientific and legal thinking was to exert a major influence on subsequent developments in Europe, dispersing in its wake the earlier teleological and religious conception of status within a collective order, an order which saw 'values' as inherent qualities of things and not as functions of men's relationships to things.

Two important elements of the moral philosophy and canon law were firstly *quid pro quo* or *justum pretium* in contracts, and secondly a prohibition – according to God's law – against charging interest on loans. Relations between men were, like relations between cosmic bodies, static and hierarchical, honour and retribution being the highest values, as it was not possible to accumulate a growing surplus in an agrarian economy. Thus, dynamics in economy and accumulation of capital were not possible until the introduction of an urban economy based on contracts, division of labour and money as payment for goods and services. In case an immediate exchange did not take place, the money claim represented the tie between creditor and tender (obligation = bond).

The technological process implies an analysis of natural laws to make possible the planning and control of nature. Within an increasingly technological world, lawmaking likewise implies the linguistic analysis and formation of precise legal concepts which delimit legal from illegal acts. Certainly, technological and economic processes can take place only within a legal structure. This is the reason why legal science gradually had to create the necessary legal concepts, institutions and rules to enable economic and technological processes to take place. Customary laws and ethics cannot cope with a dynamic economy which is dependent on an instrumental organisation (i.e. the State).

After the disruption of the Western Roman Empire, European economy was reduced to a static feudal system, and the law likewise to 'divine customs'. In the Thirteenth Century, when economic growth made urban civilisation possible, and the struggle for power between the Church and the secular rulers remained undecided, individualism emerged, as we know, and the individual human being now became the independent creator of both technology and lawmaking, a free agent with the sovereignty to change his physical and social universe.

In primitive clan communities, land ownership is collective and the inheritance goes entirely to the next generation of the clan. In the early Middle Ages, the Church had revived the private will (which was recognised in classical Roman law) as an instrument to free the dominant means of production, i.e. farm land. At first this step was mainly to the advantage of Church financing, but gradually, towards the late Medieval period, the concept of private property was introduced. In contrast to the feudal system which had prevailed until then, private property gave the owners access to use, sell, mortgage and by will dispose of land and chattels.

Concurrently with the recognition of absolute private property right, the right of individuals to bind themselves by private declarations of intent, consensus, was also recognised. The consensus between two sovereign declarations of intent created property rights or claims (contract), and society itself came to be seen as the product of a social contract.

Thanks to the development in law of systematic concepts, the tools were prepared for the construction of the elements such as contract, property, company and mortgage, required to raise capital for the technological and economic revolutions of the Nineteenth Century. The foundation was the market with its freedom of contract and the real estate mortgage system underpinned by secured rights of property. No credit would be allowed without considerable security for fulfilment of the claim; and credit secured by mortgage on property and other kinds of security offers considerable prospect of fulfilment, in legal as well as economic terms. The standardised records of rights in and encumbrances on land and property provided a high degree of reliability. This development marked an important achievement for jurisprudence and was a vital force in the technological revolution of the Nineteenth Century.

Another development of the Nineteenth Century was the refinement in law of the doctrine inherited from the late Middle Ages that 'collective entities' (convents, monasteries and churches) could acquire separate legal identity. Joint-stock companies and other limited companies first emerged during this period. Besides limited liability, these new companies also had several participants who contributed capital. These participants received dividend payments on their invested capital, but were liable only to the extent of their investment. At the same time a detailed set of rules was laid down concerning agency, i.e. the capability of a third party to sign on behalf of the company.

Mass production engendered social change. The prevailing view of society according to individualist thinkers had been one in which enlightened and rational persons were free to control their own and public matters through contract and democracy. This view was now replaced by a conflict model based on a division between capital and work. On the labour market, the unhampered individual freedom of contract was replaced by collective agreements, by which wage earners obtained security against dominant vested interests. Then, in the Twentieth Century, the constitutional state was gradually replaced by the social state, the regulatory laws and bureaucracy of which eventually led to the welfare state, under which model, the state carries political responsibility for the national economy. This model presumes a general attitude to the state as a friend. Its evil twin, however, is the high tax society in which the State is an enemy.

Events of recent decades have thus made it clear that the guarantees provided by the legal system for the fulfilment of people's social expectations cannot be realised in situations of economic, political and material stress. One cannot ask a person to do more than is within his power to do, or to do what is impossible. Since the time of Thucydides' history of the Peloponnesian War (Fifth Century BC) we have known that it is not poverty or oppression, but feelings of injustice and disappointed expectations which give rise to resistance and revolt.

The Age of Enlightenment believed that human beings possess unlimited scope for changing society by means of legislation. It was even believed that commerce could be created through the introduction of commercial laws. The Twentieth Century's legal sociologists have taught us, however, that in real life legislation can have only limited success if it is contrary to the interests of large parts of the population.

References

I. Own Works

Vertrag und Recht : privatrechtliche Abhandlungen, Copenhagen 1968.

Law and Society, Aarhus 1971.

Recht und Gesellschaft, Göttingen 1971.

Values in Law: Ideas, Principles and Rules, Copenhagen 1978.

Pluralis Juris : Towards a Relativistic Theory of Law, Aarhus 1982.

Reason and Reality, Aarhus 1986.

Fragments of Legal Cognition, Aarhus 1988.

On Justice and Law, Aarhus 1996.

'Law as a Standardizing System', *EURAS Yearbook of Standardization*. Manfred J. Holler and Esko Niskanen (eds.), vol. 1. München 1997, pp. 411-16.

II. Other References

Aubert, V. 1943. 'Om Rettsvitenskapens Logiske Grundlag', *Tidsskrift for Rettsvitenskap*, 174ff.

Austin, John 1954 (1832). *The Province of Jurisprudence Determined*. Edited by H.L.A. Hart. Oxford.

Bentzon, Viggo 1907. *Retskilderne*. Copenhagen.

Bolding, Per Olaf 1968. *Juridik och Samhällsdebatt*, Lund.

Chomsky, Noam 1957. *Syntactic Structures*, The Hague.

Dalberg-Larsen, Jørgen 1977. *Retsvidenskaben som samfundsvidenskab*, Copenhagen.

Dalberg-Larsen, Jørgen 1984. *Retsstaten, velfærdsstaten og hvad så?*, Copenhagen.

Dalberg-Larsen, Jørgen 1994. *Rettens enhed - en illusion?*, Copenhagen.

Dalberg-Larsen, Jørgen 1998. *Ret, tekst og kontekst*. Copenhagen.

Dalberg-Larsen, Jørgen og Jens Evald 1998. *Rettens ansigter.* Copenhagen.

Dewey, John 1980 (1903). *Studies in Logical Theory,* edited by J. Dewey, New York.

Dworkin, Ronald 1986. *Law's Empire,* London.

Engisch, Karl 1968. *Die Idee der Konkretiseirung in Recht und Rechtswissenschaft unserer Zeit,* 2nd ed., Heidelberg.

Evald, Jens 1997. *Retskilderne og den juridiske metode,* Copenhagen.

Fuller, Lon 1969. *The Morality of Law* , 2nd ed., New Haven.

Gadamer, Hans-Georg 1965. *Wahrheit und Methode,* 2nd ed., Tübingen.

Habermas, Jürgen 1968. *Erkenntnis und Interesse,* Frankfurt.

Hägerström, Axel 1908. *Das Prinzip der Wissenschaft. Eine logischerkenntnistheoretische Untersuchung. I. Die Realität,* Uppsala.

Hart, H.L.A. 1961. *The Concept of Law,* Oxford.

Heidegger, Martin 1935 (1927). *Sein und Zeit,* Halle a.d.S.

Hobbes, Thomas 1974. *Leviathan,* Harmondsworth.

Holmes, O.W. 1881. *The Common Law,* Boston.

Husserl, Edmund 1964. *Recht und Welt. Rechtsphilosophische Abhandlungen,* Frankfurt am Main.

Illum, Knud 1945. *Lov og Ret,* Copenhagen.

James, William 1995 (1907). *Pragmatism,* New York.

Jellinek, G. 1914. *Allgemeine Staatslehre,* Berlin.

Jhering, Rudolph von. 1872. *Der Zweck im Recht,* Leipzig.

Kelsen, Hans 1945. *General Theory of Law and State,* Cambridge.

Krawietz, Werner 1978. *Juristische Entscheidung und wissenschaftliche Erkenntnis,* Vienna.

Kruse, Fr. Vinding 1943. *Retslæren, II,* Copenhagen.

Larenz, Karl 1979. *Methodenlehre der Rechtswissenschaft,* 4th ed., Berlin.

Lassen. J. 1892. *Obligationsretten. Alm. Del,* Copenhagen.

Luhmann, Niklas 1969. *Legitimation durch Verfahren,* Neuwied am Rhein.

Lundstedt, A.V. 1930. *Obligationsbegreppet II,* Uppsala.

Løgstrup, K.E. 1956. *Den etiske fordring,* Copenhagen.

McCauly, Steward 1986. 'Private Government', *Law and the Social Sciences,* 445ff, New York.

Moore, G.E. 1903. *Principia Ethica,* Cambridge.

Møller, Ernst 1894. *Forudsætninger*, Copenhagen.

Olivecrona, K. 1939. *Law as Fact*. London.

Perelman, Chaim 1963. *Justice et raison*, Brussels.

Piaget, Jean 1936. *The Origin of Intelligence in the Child*, London.

Podgorecki, Adam 1974. *Law and Society*, London.

Pufendorf, S. von 1672. *De Jure Naturae et Gentium.*

Rawls, John 1971. *A Theory of Justice*, Cambridge.

Raz, Joseph 1970. *The Concept of a Legal System*, Oxford.

Reid, Thomas 1990 (1795). *Practical Ethics*, ed. by Knud Haakonssen. Lectures and papers from the Philosophical Works, Princeton.

Ross, Alf 1953. *Om ret og retfærdighed*, Copenhagen.

Savigny, F.C. von. 1814. *Vom Beruf unserer Zeit für Gesetzgebung und Rechtswissenschaft*, Heidelberg.

Schmitt, Carl 1934. *Über die drei Arten des rechtswissenschaftlichen Denkens*, Hamburg.

Teubner, Gunther 1983. 'Substantive and Reflexive Elements in Modern Law', *Law and Society Law Review*, vol. 17, 239.

Toulmin, S. 1986 (1950). *The Place of Reason in Ethics*, Chicago.

Ussing, Henry 1918. *Bristende Forudsætninger*, Copenhagen.

Viehweg, Theodor 1965. *Topik und Jurisprudenz*, 3rd ed., München.

Whorf, B.L. 1956. *Language, Thought and Reality: Selected Writings*, Cambridge, Mass.

Wieacker, Franz 1967. *Privatrechtsgeschichte der Neuzeit*, 2nd. ed., Göttingen.

Wittgenstein, Ludwig 1953. *Philosophical Investigations*, Oxford.

Ørsted, A.S. 1822. *Haandbog over den danske og norske Lovkyndighed*, I, Copenhagen.

INDEX

Aarnio, A. 69

Anaximenes 71

Aquinas, Thomas 25, 44, 64

Aristotle 6, 7, 18, 22, 25, 27, 44, 55, 62, 64, 69, 71, 81-82, 84-85

Attlee, C.R. 32

Aubert, V. 99

Augustus 29

Austin, J. 38

Banville, J. 25, 34-35, 37

Bentham, J. 73

Bentzon, V. 90, 110

Bergson, H. 11, 20

Blunt, A. 35

Bolding, P.O. 99

Burgess, G.F. 35

Chamberlain, N. 31

Chomsky, N. 17

Churchill, W. 31

Cicero 64, 71-72

Coase, R.H. 41

Coing, H. 68

Dalberg-Larsen, J. 69, 100

de Gaulle, C. 32

Descartes 10, 18-19, 82

Dewey, J. 11, 20

Dilthey 68

Durell, L. 24

Dworkin, R. 39-40, 52

Einstein, A. 62

Eisenhower, D.D. 42

Engisch, K. 40, 69

Esser, J. 68

Fichte. J.G. 53, 56

Freud, S. 24

From, F. 21, 29

Fuller, L. 39, 48

Gadamer 67-68, 73-74

Gaius 71, 81

Galileo 10, 18, 82

Gide, A. 24

Goering, H.W. 32

Gorgias 71

Grotius, H. 44, 64, 72

Habermas, J. 52, 54, 69, 100

Hägerström, A. 11, 15, 20, 57, 90

Hart, H.L.A. 11, 38-39, 48, 84

Hegel, G.W.F. 10, 19, 84

Heidegger, M. 20, 54, 73, 68

Hindenburg, P. von 31

Hitler, A. 31

Hobbes, T. 38, 44

Holberg, L. 28

Holmes, O.W. 38

Honoré, T. 84

Hume, D. 5, 10, 19, 56, 72, 79-80, 89, 107

Husserl, E. 11, 20

Ihering, R. von 10, 72, 103

Illum, K. 79, 90, 96
James, W. 11, 20
Jaynes, J. 14
Jellinek, G. 45
Jung, C.G. 24
Justinian 71
Kant, I. 5-6, 19, 27, 44-45, 56, 72, 79-80, 88-89, 103, 107
Kelsen, H. 20, 43, 47, 51, 99, 100-1, 107
Kierkegaard, S. 53
Kruse, F.V. 90
Larenz, K. 69
Lassen, J. 95
Løgstrup, K.E. 48
Luhmann, N. 41, 52, 100
Lundstedt, A.V. 90, 101
MacCormick, N. 69
Maclean, D. 35
Madsen, S.A. 37
Massie, A. 25, 29, 36
McCauly, S. 101
Møller, E. 96
Montesquieu, Baron de 44, 56, 84
Moore, G.E. 11, 19
Musil, R. 29
Newton, I. 35
Nielsen, J. 15
Nietzsche, F.W. 10, 72
Nixon, R. 29
Olivecrona, K. 57
Ørsted, A.S. 44, 56, 89

Peczenik, A. 69
Perelman, C. 52, 69
Pétain, H.P. 31
Petersen, S. 28
Philby, K. 35
Piaget, J. 17
Plato 7, 25, 71, 83
Podgorecki, A. 100
Pompeius 26
Posner, R. 41
Poussin, N. 37
Pufendorf, S. von 64-65
Rawls, J. 52
Raz, J. 40
Reid, T. 11, 20
Ringgaard, K. 16
Roosevelt, F.D. 42
Ross, A. 20, 57, 74, 90, 99
Rousseau, J.J. 107
Savigny, F.C. von 44
Scavenius, E. 31
Schmitt, K. 101
Schopenhauer, A. 10, 72
Storr, A. 25
Teubner, G. 52, 100
Thatcher, M. 32
Tieck, L. 33
Toulmin, S. 69
Ussing, H. 90-91, 95, 97, 104
Viehweg, T. 69
Weber, M. 100-1
Whorf, L. 16
Wieacker, F. 68
Wittgenstein, B.L. 20